A QUIP OFF THE OLD BLOCK

One morning Annette went into her mother's bathroom and remarked on the size of her tummy.

"Well, dear, you see Daddy has given me a little baby."

The girl rushed into the bedroom and cried, "Daddy, did you give Mummy a little baby?"

"Er . . . er . . . yes, I did," said the father.

"Well," said the daughter, "she's eaten it!"

THE LAST OFFICIAL
SMART KIDS JOKE BOOK

THE *LAST* OFFICIAL POLISH JOKE BOOK
THE OFFICIAL GOLFERS JOKE BOOK
THE OFFICIAL SMART KIDS/DUMB
  PARENTS JOKE BOOK
THE OFFICIAL RELIGIOUS/NOT SO
  RELIGIOUS JOKE BOOK
THE OFFICIAL DEMOCRAT/REPUBLICAN
  JOKE BOOK
MORE THE OFFICIAL POLISH/ITALIAN
  JOKE BOOK
THE OFFICIAL BLACK FOLKS/WHITE FOLKS
  JOKE BOOK
THE OFFICIAL VIRGINS/SEX MANIACS
  JOKE BOOK
THE OFFICIAL JEWISH/IRISH JOKE BOOK
THE OFFICIAL POLISH/ITALIAN JOKE BOOK

AND IN HARDCOVER

THE COMPLETE BOOK OF ETHNIC HUMOR
HOW THE GREAT COMEDY WRITERS
  CREATE LAUGHTER
THE GREAT COMEDIANS TALK ABOUT
  COMEDY

THE *Last* OFFICIAL SMART KIDS JOKE BOOK

LARRY WILDE

Illustrations by Ron Wing

BANTAM BOOKS
TORONTO · NEW YORK · LONDON · SYDNEY

THE LAST OFFICIAL SMART KIDS JOKE BOOK
A Bantam Book / October 1983

ISBN 0-553-23587-7

Published simultaneously in the United States and Canada

Bantam Books are published by Bantam Books, Inc. Its
trademark, consisting of the words ''Bantam Books'' and the
portrayal of a rooster, is Registered in U.S. Patent and Trademark Office and in other countries. Marca Registrada. Bantam Books, Inc., 666 Fifth Avenue, New York, New York
10103.

PRINTED IN THE UNITED STATES OF AMERICA

O   0 9 8 7 6 5 4 3 2 1

DEDICATION

For Fred Klein:
The wittiest, brightest,
smartest kid in publishing.

CONTENTS

GOOFY GIGGLES

"Sir, the enemy are advancing as thick as peas in a pod."

"Okay, lieutenant. Shell them."

*   *   *

When is it bad luck to have a black cat follow you?

When you're a mouse!

*   *   *

"I keep seeing spots in front of my eyes all day long."

"Have you seen an oculist?"

"No. Just spots."

*   *   *

If a bakery explodes in your face, what might you see?

A Napoleon blown apart, of course!

*   *   *

What did the short-order cook give his girlfriend when they became engaged?
A 14-carat onion ring.

*   *   *

Where was the Declaration of Independence signed?
At the bottom.

*   *   *

If you see two monsters, two werewolves, and two witches in a room together, what should you do?
Hope it's a Halloween Party.

*   *   *

JOLLY GREEN GIANT TOMBSTONE

Rest in Peas

*   *   *

Why did the lobster get a divorce from his wife?
Because he was married to a crab.

*   *   *

ne stayed out in the sun too long?
A baked bean.

* * *

Why does the Indian wear feathers in
his hair?
To keep his wigwam.

* * *

Did you hear about the new invention
to help the hearing of deaf fish?
It's called a herring aid.

* * *

What do you get when you cross a
chicken and a bell?
An alarm cluck.

* * *

What is a dead giveaway?
A will.

* * *

There once was a lady named Perkins,
Who had a great fondness for gherkins.
    She went out to a tea
    And ate twenty-three,
Which pickled her internal workin's.

3

Alice: I own 186 goldfish.
Hilda: Where do you keep them?
Alice: In the bathroom.
Hilda: What do you do when you want to take a bath?
Alice: I blindfold them.

*   *   *

What sort of boats do vampires prefer?
Blood vessels.

*   *   *

SWEATER

*A garment worn by a small child
when his mother feels chilly.*

*   *   *

What is the first thing a farmer must remember?
Never try to milk a bull.

*   *   *

Where can you find girls who won't neck in cars?
The woods are full of them.

*   *   *

What did the near-sighted porcupine say when it backed into a cactus?

"Pardon me, honey."

* * *

Little Kurt fell off his bicycle and cut his knee. His mother bathed and dressed the wound, and then gave the boy a pill to soothe him. After he swallowed it, Kurt asked, "How will the pill know which leg to go down?"

* * *

There once was a kid named O'Neill,
Who rode on the high Ferris wheel;
But then halfway around
He looked down at the ground—
That cost him a ten-dollar meal.

* * *

What did the mama broom and the papa broom say to the baby broom?

"Go to sweep."

* * *

What did the big toe say to the little toe?

"Don't look now, but there's a heel following us."

A horse walked into a restaurant, sat down at a table and, when Weinstock the waiter came over, gave his order.

"I want a New York sirloin, three-inches thick, done medium rare. On top of it, I want two-dozen fried oysters and a small portion of boiled beets. On the side, I want a Maui onion, some potato Perogi, a sliced banana and a bottle of Perrier."

Weinstock brought the horse's order. After he finished eating, the horse said to the waiter, "Don't you think it's a bit odd? I mean me, a horse, coming into a restaurant and ordering a steak with all the trimmings like that?"

"Not at all," replied the waiter. "I like it that way myself."

*   *   *

What did one tonsil say to the other tonsil?

"Better get dressed. The doctor's taking us out tonight."

*   *   *

What's the difference between a fly and a mosquito?

You can't sew a zipper on a mosquito.

*   *   *

Karate Expert: What hurts worse than a karate chop in the chest?

Alexander: One of my mother's pork chops in the stomach.

*   *   *

What is the best thing to take when you are rundown?

The number of the car that hit you.

*   *   *

Why is it impossible for a boy who lisps to believe in young ladies?

Because with him every miss is a myth.

*   *   *

What is the difference between a cat and a frog?

A cat has only nine lives—a frog croaks every minute.

*   *   *

Peggy: There were three men in a boat with four cigarettes but no matches. What did they do?

Wally: I give up. What?

Peggy: They threw out one cigarette and made the boat a cigarette lighter.

*   *   *

Four men fell into the water but only three of them got their hair wet. Why?

One of them was bald.

*   *   *

Did you hear about the lark that went off with a woodpecker, and learned that love is a many-splintered thing?

*   *   *

When the papa bee stung the mama bee, she had a little bumble from heaven.

*   *   *

line are jumping backwards?
A receding hare line.

*   *   *

Waterford: You sold me this canary yesterday.
Pet-shop man: Well?
Waterford: Well, it's lame.
Pet-shop man: What do you want, a singer or a dancer?

*   *   *

Who said, "I'm going to give you a big squeeze when I meet you on the bridge tonight?"
A toothbrush . . . talking to the toothpaste.

*   *   *

SIGN IN A CLOCK REPAIR SHOP WINDOW

Cuckoo Clocks Psychoanalyzed Free

*   *   *

What do they call folks who never return borrowed books?
Bookkeepers.

What's the difference between an Irish-man frozen to death and a Scotsman at the North Pole?

One is kilt with the cold—the other cold with the kilt.

* * *

Two strawberries were cooking in a pot, and it got hotter and more uncomfortable every moment. Said one to the other, "You know, if us two hadn't been found in the same bed, we wouldn't be in this jam now."

* * *

Kids have the unique ability to create special names for the handicapped. Here are some unusual monikers being used today:

What do you call a guy who has two stumps for legs?
Neal.

What do you call a guy with no arms or legs floating in a swimming pool?
Bob.

What do you call a one-legged girl skier?
Eileen.

11

*   *   *

Father: Where's tonight's paper?

Son: I wrapped the garbage in it and threw it out.

Father: I wanted to see it.

Son: There wasn't much to see. Only an orange peel, two lamb-chop bones and some coffee grounds.

*   *   *

Little Freddie was given an orange by a lady visitor.

"What do you say to the nice lady?" his mother prompted.

Igor replied, "Peel it."

*   *   *

What is the difference between a cloud and a boy getting a spanking?

The cloud pours with rain and the boy roars with pain.

*   *   *

SIGN IN BAKERY WINDOW

Cheesecake Like Mother Used to Buy

*   *   *

Karl Kangaroo and his wife Kathy were on their way home from a neighbor's barbecue. On every third hop Baby Kangaroo popped out of his mother's pouch. Finally the Father stopped and said to his wife, "Why don't you tuck the little one farther down into your pouch so he won't keep popping out?"

"It isn't his fault," replied Kathy Kangaroo. "I have the hiccups!"

* * *

What is the difference between a running girl and a running dog?

One wears a skirt, the other pants.

* * *

If you were locked in a room that had in it only a bed and a calendar, what would you do for food?

Get water from the bed springs and dates from the calendar.

* * *

How do you tell where a miser lives?

There's a parking meter on the chimney at Christmas.

* * *

Bill: Are you fishing?
Will: Nah, I'm drowning worms.

Beggar: Mister, can you spare a thousand dollars for a cup of coffee?

Kingston: A thousand dollars! How many people do you think are going to give you a thousand dollars?

Beggar: Well, if only a couple did, I could quit begging.

*   *   *

Why are there so few men with whiskers in heaven?

Because most men get in by a close shave.

*   *   *

How can you make an Irishman's tongue turn black?

Drop a bottle of brandy on a freshly tarred road.

*   *   *

Why did the little boy tiptoe past the medicine chest?

He was afraid he'd awaken the sleeping pills.

*   *   *

*   *   *

SIGN ON THE GATE OF A NEW FACTORY IN CALIFORNIA

Men wanted to work on nuclear-
fissionable isotope counters and
three-phase photosynthesizers.
No experience necessary.

*   *   *

What happens to a mother who doesn't
know cold cream from putty?
Her windows fall out.

*   *   *

Two passengers on a train:
"Excuse me, does this train stop at
Aurora?"
"Yes, just watch me and get off one
station before me."

*   *   *

"Ha, ha, ha! I sure put one over on the
railroad today."
"How?"
"I bought a round-trip ticket to Miami
and I'm never coming back."

*   *   *

Hubbard walked up to the box office at a movie theater. He tapped on the ticket window, and growled at the cashier, "You people advertise popular prices, and yet you charge $5 to get in and see the show. You people must be crazy. Do you call $5 a popular price?"

"Well," replied the cashier, "we like it."

*   *   *

"Did you fill in that blank yet?"
"What blank?"
"The one between your ears?"

*   *   *

What did the painter say to the wall?
"One more crack like that and I'll plaster you."

*   *   *

Why was the little shoe so sad?
Because his mother was a loafer and his father was a sneaker.

*   *   *

What did the mayonnaise say to the refrigerator?
"Close the door, I'm dressing."

Mrs. Kowalski was going out for the day. She locked the house and tacked a note for the milkman on the door:

NOBODY HOME.
DON'T LEAVE ANYTHING.

That night when she returned Mrs. Kowalski found her door broken open and her house ransacked. On the note she had left, she found the following message added:

THANKS! WE HAVEN'T LEFT MUCH.

*   *   *

What is the difference between a counterfeit five-dollar bill and an angry rabbit?
One is bad money and the other is a mad bunny.

*   *   *

SIGN ON A GARBAGE TRUCK

Your garbage is our bread and butter.

*   *   *

It was getting close to December 25th and Mrs. Beck casually asked her ten-year-old daughter, "What would you like for Christmas?"

"A mirror, Mommy."

"My goodness. Why?"

"Because," sighed the girl, "I'm getting too big to make up in the doorknob."

Baldwin went into a costume shop and said, "I'm going to a Halloween party and I'd like to rent a costume. What have you got?"

"How about a pirate costume?" suggested the owner. "I can give you a knit cap, a silk shirt, satin pants, leather boots, and a real sword for $50."

"I didn't want to spend that much. You got anything cheaper?"

"You can have the cap, a sweatshirt, plain pants, boots and a *rubber* sword for $25."

"That's still too expensive," complained Baldwin.

"How about the cap, pants, sneakers and a *cardboard* sword for $10?" asked the owner.

"No, that's still too high."

"Well then, for $5 I can give you a broomstick and a can of red paint."

"What can I do with that?" asked Baldwin.

"Put the broomstick in your mouth, pour the paint over your head, and go as a candy apple!"

*   *   *

Why did Mama Flea look so sad?

Because all her children were going to the dogs.

*   *   *

Sally and Freida, two flies, met at a kitchen table.

"How's the new baby?" asked Sally Fly.

"Very restless," replied her friend Frieda Fly. "I had to walk the ceiling all night with him."

*   *   *

Little Huntley stood in a department store near the escalator watching the moving handrail.

"Something wrong, son?" inquired the security guard.

"Nope," replied the boy, "just waiting for my chewing gum to come back."

*   *   *

Malcolm and Boyd, two mosquitos, were chatting.

"What makes you so happy?" asked Malcolm.

"I just passed my screen test," replied Boyd.

*   *   *

Trent Turtle: I want to get a gift for my wife for her birthday. Got any suggestions?

Tab Turtle: How about a people-neck sweater?

*   *   *

Mrs. Mouse was taking her babies out for a little stroll when they were startled by a large cat.

"Bow-wow!" shouted Mrs. Mouse and the cat turned and ran away.

"See, children," said the mother, "how important it is to speak another language!"

*   *   *

Ken and Otis were sitting on a tree stump.

"What do raccoons eat?" asked Ken.

"They eat anything they can find," answered Otis.

"But what if they can't find anything?"

"Then they eat something else."

*   *   *

Mrs. Gnu was waiting for her husband to come home and punish their little boy.

When Papa Gnu finally arrived, his wife said, "Our son was very bad today, and I want you to punish him."

"Oh, no, I won't do it," said Papa Gnu. "You'll have to learn to paddle your own gnu."

*   *   *

Lloyd the leopard stopped to see an optometrist.

"Every time I look at my wife, I see spots before my eyes," he said.

"What do you expect?" answered the optometrist. "You're a leopard, aren't you?"

"Yes," said Lloyd, "but my wife is a zebra."

*　　*　　*

Scarlett the skunk was worried because she had trouble keeping track of her two children. They were named In and Out. And whenever In was in, Out was out. But if Out was in, then In was out.

One day Scarlett called Out in to her and told him to go out and bring In in. So Out went out and, in no time at all, brought In in.

"Wonderful!" said Mrs. Skunk. "How, in all this great forest, could you find In in so short a time?"

"It was easy," said Out. *"In stinct."*

*　　*　　*

A ferocious lion killed and ate a bull. Afterwards he felt so wonderful, he pranced all over and just roared and roared. A hunter heard the lion roar, and shot him dead.

Moral: When you're full of bull, you'd better keep your mouth shut.

The telephone on an editor's desk rang insistently.

He picked it up and a voice said, "You're all wet about the high cost of living. My wife and I live real good eating everything we like, on less than two dollars a week."

"Two dollars a week!" cried the editor. "I can't believe it! Please tell me how you do it and, to make sure I get the story straight, please speak louder."

"I can't speak louder," came the answer. "I'm a goldfish."

BARNYARD BOFFS

A speeding Buick ran over one of Farmer Middleton's hogs.

"Don't worry," said the driver of the car, "I'll replace your hog."

"You can't," said the farmer. "You ain't fat enough."

*   *   *

Farmer: That new man I hired yesterday doesn't know much about farming.
Wife: Why do you say that?
Farmer: He saw some milk bottles behind the barn and ran to me shouting he'd found a cow's nest.

As a motorist drove away from a farmer's orchard he shouted, "We picked some of your apples. We didn't think you'd mind."

"Not at all," yelled the farmer after them. "I picked some of your car's tools from the trunk. I didn't think you'd mind, either."

*   *   *

Riggs and Crawford, two Kentucky farmers, met in town at the general store.

"I made sure not to be caught by any drought this summer," said Riggs.

"How'd you manage that?" asked Crawford.

"I planted onions and potatoes next to each other. That way, the onions'll make the potatoes' eyes water and that'll irrigate my soil."

*   *   *

They strolled down the lane together,
The sky was studded with stars.
They reached the gate in silence,
And he lifted up the bars.
She neither smiled nor thanked him,
For indeed she knew not how.
For he was just a farmer boy, and she—
A Jersey cow.

An older chicken was strolling around the barn with a younger hen having an afternoon chat.

"Let me give you some advice," said the old hen.

"What is it?" said the young chicken.

"An egg a day keeps the ax away."

*   *   *

Reggie the rooster and Trina the turkey were in the barnyard complaining about their low station in life. Reggie went on for more than an hour about the many abuses he was forced to suffer. Finally it was Trina's turn.

"Listen," she began, "You think you got troubles? Consider the poor turkey. First somebody gives him such a hit in the neck, his head flies off the handle. Then they tear off the wings, break his legs, knock the stuffings out of him, cut him to pieces and, as if all that weren't enough, they pick on him for weeks after."

*   *   *

Did you hear about the two farmers who had an argument about a vegetable?

One said it was celery, and the other said it was cauliflower.

It turned out to be a rhubarb.

*   *   *

Jason Vertucca, Sebastapol's football fanatic, gets kicks out of this fun fooler:

Elwood punted his football, and it landed across the fence and in a chicken yard.

The rooster was impressed with its size and crowed to the hens, "Ladies, I don't like to complain, but I wish you'd come over and take a look at what's being done in other yards."

*   *   *

City Visitor: Are the mosquitoes tame around here?

Farmer: Are they tame? Why, they'll eat right out of your hand.

*   *   *

Leonard, a city boy, was on a farm and saw the milking of a cow for the first time.

"Now you know where milk comes from, don't you?" asked the farmhand.

"Sure!" exclaimed Leonard. "You give the cow some breakfast—food and water— then you drain the crankcase."

*   *   *

Little Cindy was visiting her grandfather's farm for the first time. "Grandpa," she asked, "What kind of cow is that?"

"It's a Jersey cow."

"How can you tell? It's not wearing any license plates."

*   *   *

"How do baby chickens dance?"
"Chick to chick, naturally."

*   *   *

"Down on the farm," said the farmer, "we go to bed with the chickens."

"Well," said the city dweller, "in town we'd rather sleep in our own beds."

*　　*　　*

Hiram, the new hired hand, spoke right up to his employer. "Your farming methods are terribly old-fashioned. I doubt if you'll get ten pounds of apples from that tree."

"I doubt it too," said the farmer. "It's a peach tree."

*　　*　　*

Geraldine, the hired girl, was sent down to the stream to fetch a pail of water, but she just stood there gazing at the water, apparently lost in thought.

"What's she waiting for?" asked the farmer's wife.

"I dunno," replied the farmer. "Maybe she hasn't seen a pailful she likes yet."

*　　*　　*

McAlister was driving on a Georgia country road when he jammed on the brakes and shouted to a farmer, "Why are you running that steamroller over your field?"

"I'm gonna raise me a crop of mashed potatoes," explained the farmer.

Jeff Bari, Gualala's best ball player, gets belly laughs with this beaut:

Harris was traveling across the country all by himself in a balloon. While passing over a California farm he spotted a farmer bailing hay.

"Halloo!" shouted Harris down to the farmer. "Where am I?"

The farmer looked up and shook his head.

"You can't fool me, feller," he retorted, "You're right up there in that little basket."

Veterinarian:	Your cow must take a table-spoon of this medicine twice a day.
Farmer:	But the cow don't have no tablespoons. She drinks out of a pail.

* * *

Stuart and Mead, two farmers, met after Sunday church services.

"Say," asked Stuart. "What'd you give your mule when he was sick?"

"Turpentine," answered Mead.

Two weeks passed and they met again.

"What did you say you gave your mule when he was sick?"

"Well, I gave my mule turpentine, and it killed him."

"Killed mine too."

* * *

What do you get if you cross a centipede with a turkey?

Fewer fights over who gets the drumsticks.

* * *

A mother hen had been observing the undisciplined behavior of her youngest chick with obvious disapproval.

"If your father could see you now," she cackled disgustedly, "he'd turn over in his gravy."

*   *   *

Hazel and Sunflower, two Jersey cows, were looking over the wall at the passing traffic when they saw a large tanker passing with this sign in bold letters:

TRY OUR TUBERCULIN-TESTED MILK
PASTEURIZED—STERILIZED—
HOMOGENIZED

Hazel turned to her neighbor and sighed, "Oh, Sunflower, it makes you feel kind of inadequate, doesn't it?"

*   *   *

Farmer: I heard a mule kicked you yesterday. Where did he kick you?

New Hand: Well, if my head was in New York and my feet in California, he would've kicked me in Chicago.

*   *   *

La Jolla's happy animal lover Helen Morris tells this witty tale about a wittle wabbit:

The farmer's wife opened her refrigerator and, lo, there was a rabbit inside. "What are you doing here?" she asked.

"Isn't this a Westinghouse?" replied the rabbit.

The woman said, "Yes."

"Well, I'm westing."

"I crossed a cow with a kangaroo."

"What did you get?"

"I'm not sure, but you have to milk it on a pogo stick."

*　　*　　*

Farmer Shelton and his wife were having breakfast.

"When are you going to fix that pasture fence?" asked Mrs. Shelton.

"Next week when Cyrus comes home from college on vacation."

"But what will the boy know about fixing a fence?"

"He ought to know a heap," said Shelton. "He wrote me that he's been taking fencing lessons at school."

*　　*　　*

Farmer Kelton needed another hand and he interviewed a young fellow.

"Can you tell me how long cows should be milked?"

"They should be milked the same as short ones, naturally," replied the fellow.

*　　*　　*

"Is Ballpoint really the name of your pig?"

"No, that's just his pen name."

Did you hear about the two shepherds who formed a partnership?

In the springtime they shear and shear alike.

*   *   *

Zeke: Where's that mule you were gonna sell me?
Clem: He got better.

*   *   *

Mother Rabbit to her baby: "A magician pulled you out of a hat—now stop asking questions!"

*   *   *

Nick Zezas, the Buffalo, Wyoming cattle baron, beams over this bubbling tailwagger:

Caldwell was visiting a ranch and asking lots of questions about the animals. "Say," he asked the rancher, "why doesn't that cow have horns?"

"Well," said the rancher, "cows don't have horns for many reasons. Some have 'em removed, some kinds of cows never growed them, and some get them when they're old. That particular cow don't have none because he's a horse."

Anthony Seidman, the Sherman Oaks Ferrari fanatic, finds fun in this frolicker:

Colson was driving through an Arkansas farming community and noticed a pig with a wooden leg, walking with crutches. Colson jammed on the brakes and rushed over to ask Farmer Bartlett about the unusual razorback.

"That there piggy is practically a house pet," explained Bartlett. "Couple months ago it was in the pickup with my wife when she skidded off the road and was knocked unconscious. The porker kept oinkin' and squealin' 'till it attracted the attention of a passerby. Saved my pore wife's life."

"That's really amazing," agreed Colson.

"Then, just last week my youngest was drownin' in the lake and that there hog swum out and pulled him to shore."

"Oh, that's wonderful!" said the motorist. "But why is one of his leg's made of wood?"

"Well," said the farmer, "he's such a nice pig we can't eat him all at one time."

One morning Hans and Herman, two German billy goats, came upon an old, rusting auto. After feasting on it for two days, they went back to the farm to tell the other goats.

"Ve don't believe you ate a whole car," one of the goats protested.

"Vell, ve did!" cried Hans.

"Vat kind of car vass it?" demanded the disbeliever.

"Let's see now," pondered Herman. "Oh, yes, I remember—it vass a Ford V-8!"

CANNIBAL CRACKS

"Shall I boil the new missionary?" asked the cannibal cook.

"Boil him?" cried the chief. "Of course not. He's a friar."

* * *

A missionary visiting a certain tribe in Africa asked the chief, "Do you people know anything about religion?"

"Well," explained the chief, "we got a little taste of it when the last missionary was here."

45

As he was placed in a huge pot to cook, the missionary asked, "In this day and age how can you still believe in cannibalism?"

"Listen," said the King, "I'm a Cambridge man—but tradition is tradition."

"You went to Cambridge? And you speak perfect English. Yet . . . yet . . . you still eat your fellow man?"

"Absolutely," said the King, "only now I use a knife and fork."

* * *

CANNIBAL

An inhabitant of Africa who lives on other people. In America, they are called "relatives."

* * *

A missionary, deep in the jungle, came upon a witch doctor who was pounding heavily on a drum.

"What is going on?" asked the frightened missionary.

"We have no water," explained the cannibal.

"I see," said the religious leader. "So you're praying for rain?"

"No," said the witch doctor, "I'm sending for the plumber."

* * *

The tribe had eaten the missionary and had thoroughly enjoyed him. Next day one of the cannibals, poking about the deadman's belongings, found a magazine. He began tearing out pictures of men, women, and children, cramming them into his mouth and chewing them.

The chief watched him for awhile and then asked, "Say, is that dehydrated stuff any good?"

* * *

Hunter: Good Lord! Here comes a bunch of cannibals!

Guide: Sh! Don't get yourself in a stew.

* * *

Denton was washed ashore after many days on the open sea. The island on which he landed was inhabited by savage cannibals who tied him, dazed and exhausted, to a thick stake. They then proceeded to cut his arms with their spears and drink his blood.

This went on for several days, until the castaway could stand no more. He yelled for the cannibal king and shouted, "You can kill me if you want to, but this torture with the spears has got to stop. Damn it, I'm tired of being stuck for the drinks."

Did you hear about the cannibal who bought his wife a Valentine's Day gift?

A five-pound box of Farmer's Fannies.

*   *   *

Then there was the crooked crematorium operator who sold the ashes to cannibals as Instant People.

*   *   *

Timbuku stopped by a friend's hut to admire his new possession—a large refrigerator.

"What's its capacity?" asked Timbuku.

"I really don't know," replied the other cannibal, "but at least it holds the two men who brought it."

*   *   *

Two society leaders in a cannibal tribe were discussing marital problems.

"I don't know what to make of my husband these days," said one woman.

"Don't let that bother you," offered the other. "I'll send over my new book of recipes."

*   *   *

What do cannibals eat for dessert?

Bawanna splits.

CANNIBAL

A man who goes into a restaurant and orders the waiter.

*   *   *

The cannibal-chief's daughter came home in high, good spirits from a holiday at the seashore.

"You meet a handsome man on the beach?" asked a girlfriend.

"Did I?" she replied. "But wait! You don't have to take my word for it. I've got him right here in my suitcase!"

*   *   *

A cannibal warrior felt depressed and went to his witch doctor. After listening to him for some time, the primitive medical man said, "The trouble with you is that you're just fed up with people."

*   *   *

Two sailors were shipwrecked on a desert island.

"You needn't be nervous," said the first sailor looking at the dancing natives, "they're only singing a welcome."

"Welcome my eye," said the second. "They're saying grace."

The cannibal king and his son Laguma were hunting in the jungle when they came upon a shapely maiden bathing in a stream.

"Look," whispered the young man, "there's our breakfast. I'm hungry."

"No, we don't want to eat her," objected the king.

"But I'm hungry," said Laguma.

"Now listen to me," replied the father. "You crawl up slowly toward her while I sneak around the other side, and we'll capture her. Then we'll take her home, and eat your mother."

CANNIBAL CANTATA

"I shouldn't have eaten that missionary,"
Said the cannibal with a frown.
"For this gastritis tells me
You can't keep a good man down."

*   *   *

The Irish missionary was preaching to the African tribe. "And I say to you that you must love your fellow men!"

"Gumba Mooli," shrieked the natives.

"White man and black man must learn to cooperate."

"Gumba Mooli," chanted the crowd.

The missionary told the chief how pleased he was with the reception.

"I am glad, O man of Ireland," said the chief, "but be careful as you pass my cattle that you do not step into the Gumba Mooli."

*   *   *

ANT EATER

A cannibal who eats
his mother's sister.

*   *   *

Two cannibals entered a cocktail lounge, sat at the bar, and ordered two martinis.

The barmaid served the drinks, but eyed her two customers with distaste.

One of the cannibals became offended at her attitude, leaped over the bar, and devoured the woman. He returned to his seat and promptly fell asleep.

Three hours later, he awoke and said to his friend, "I don't know what made me so sleepy!"

"Dope!" cried the other cannibal. "It was the bar-bitch-you-ate!"

*   *   *

"What's your job?" asked the cannibal chief.

"I am editor of the city paper," replied the captive.

"Good," said the cannibal, smiling. "Tomorrow you be editor-in-chief."

*   *   *

Cannibal King: What am I having for lunch?
Cook: Two old maids.
Cannibal King: Ugh! Leftovers again.

*   *   *

CANNIBAL

*A guy who loves his fellow man
—with gravy*

An African chieftain flew to New York for a visit and was interviewed at the airport by newsmen.

"Did you have a good flight?" asked the man from *The Daily News*.

The chief made a series of strange noises— *honk, oink, screech, whistle, z-z-z*— then added in perfect English, "Yes, very pleasant, indeed."

"How long are you going to stay?" he was asked by the *Post* reporter.

Out came the string of weird noises and the words, "About three weeks."

"Tell me, Chief," inquired the *Times* reporter, "where did you learn to speak such flawless English?"

Again the screeches and whistles. Then the chief said, "Shortwave radio."

FAMILY FUNNIES

"You have an awfully good stomach, haven't you, mama?"

"Why do you say that?"

"I heard daddy tell my baby-sitter you swallow everything he tells you."

*   *   *

"Roger, dear, come kiss our new housekeeper!"

"No," said the boy, "I don't dare to, I'm afraid."

"But why, darling?"

"Dad kissed her yesterday and she slapped his face."

A father decided it was time to teach the facts of life to Irwin, his ten-year-old son. He sat the boy down and, rather nervously, explained all about the bees and the flowers.

When he finished, the father suggested that the boy pass on this information to his eight-year-old brother.

Irwin went to his younger brother's room and said to him, "You know what married people do when they want to have kids? Dad says that bees and flowers do the same thing."

* * *

Wilbur, age eight, was asked by his grandfather, "What is the first thing you notice about a girl?"

"Well," replied the boy, "that all depends on which direction she's facing."

* * *

Kevin, while doing his homework, said, "Hey, Dad, what is the distance to the nearest star?"

"I really don't know," answered his father.

"Well, I hope you'll feel sorry tomorrow when I'm getting punished for your ignorance."

* * *

"You're always asking questions," said Leo's father. "I'd like to know what would have happened if I'd asked as many questions when I was a boy."

"Maybe," said Leo, "you'd have been able to answer some of mine."

* * *

Duane: That problem you helped me with last night was all wrong, Dad.
Father: All wrong, was it. Well, I'm sorry.
Duane: Don't worry about it. None of the other daddies got it right, either.

* * *

Uncle Ralph came for dinner and before leaving he gave his nephew five dollars. "Now be careful with that money, Calvin," he said. "Remember the saying, 'A fool and his money are soon parted.'"

"Yes, Uncle," replied the boy, "but I want to thank you for parting with it, just the same."

* * *

Visiting Uncle: If you're really good, Paul, I'll give you this bright new quarter.
Paul: Haven't you got a dirty old dollar?

"Everett," screamed his mother, "you've been fighting again, and this time you've lost all your teeth."

"No, I haven't, mom," protested the boy. "I got 'em right here in my pocket."

* * *

Mickey came home from school with two black eyes. "You've been fighting again," said his mother. "Why didn't you count to ten before getting angry, like I've always told you to do?"

"I did," said the boy, "but the other guy's mother told him to count up to five!"

* * *

"Dad, can you write in the dark?"

"Of course, son. What do you want me to write?"

"Your name on my report card."

* * *

Steve asked his father, "Did your dad spank you when you were a little boy?"

"He did."

"And did his father before him spank him, too?"

"Yes, Son, he did."

"You know, Dad, with your cooperation, we could end this inherited rowdyism."

*   *   *

"Dad?"

"Yes, son."

"It says here, 'A man is known by the company he keeps.' Is that so?"

"Yes, son."

"Well, if a good man keeps company with a bad man, is the good man bad because he keeps company with the bad man, or is the bad man good because he keeps company with the good man?"

*   *   *

Dalton was shopping at Macy's with his small daughter, when she suddenly pulled on his coat sleeve and said, "Daddy, I gotta go."

"In a few minutes, dear," replied the father.

"I gotta go now," she insisted in a very loud voice.

To avoid a scene, a saleslady stepped forward and said, "That's all right, sir, I'll take her."

The saleslady and the little girl hurried off hand in hand. When they returned, Dalton asked his daughter, "Did you thank the nice lady for being so kind?"

"Why should I thank her?" retorted the child. "She had to go, too."

*   *   *

Harry T. Browne, Chicago's famed photographer, favors this fanciful dash of frivolity:

Wesley's mother was buying fruit and vegetables from Marino's Market. As Wesley stared at the cherries, Marino told him to take a handful. But Wesley said no.

"What's a matta? You no like-a da cherry?" asked the Italian.

"Yes," replied Wesley.

"Then go ahead and take some."

The boy still hesitated, whereupon Marino put a generous handful in the boy's cap. As they walked away the mother asked, "Why didn't you take the cherries when he told you to?"

" 'Cause his hand was bigger'n mine," said the youngster.

*   *   *

Father   (to son who has stolen candy from the table):   Put back that candy at once.

Son: Hush, Dad! Don't let all these people know how badly I have been brought up!

*   *   *

A mother proudly introduced her son to a charity-committee friend. "This is my son, Drexel, Mrs. Crane. Isn't he a bright little boy?"

The youngster, quite accustomed to being shown off in public, purred, "What was that clever thing I said yesterday, Mother?"

*   *   *

"Arnold, why don't you take your little sister with you when you go fishing today?"

"No," said the boy. "Last time she tagged along I didn't catch a fish."

"I'm sure she'll be quiet this time," said his mother.

"It wasn't the noise," said the youngster. "She ate the bait."

*   *   *

Alice ran to her mother crying, "Look! Craig put this frog in my bed!"

"Craig!" called the mother. "Why did you do that?"

"Well," said the boy. "I couldn't find a snake."

* * *

Mother: Howard, get your little sister's hat out of that puddle.

Howard: I can't, Mom, she's got it strapped too tight under her chin.

* * *

An elderly Connecticut farmer who had little patience with children finally surrendered to the charms of his attractive, young housekeeper, the mother of a ten-year-old brat.

Soon after the marriage, she went to New York to do some shopping. Upon her return she asked her son how he got along with his new father.

"Okay," said the youngster, "every morning he took me out on the lake in a rowboat and let me swim back."

"Heavens that's a long distance to swim!"

"Oh, I made it all right," said the boy. "Only trouble I had was getting out of the burlap bag."

*   *   *

"What's your younger brother wailing about?" demanded a father.

The older son explained, "He's just crying because I'm eating my pie and won't give him any."

"Is his pie finished?" asked the father.

"It is," said the boy, "and he wailed while I was eating that, too."

*   *   *

As the hero in the play slapped the heroine, a small voice in the audience was heard to ask, "Mother, why doesn't she hit him back like you do Daddy?"

*   *   *

Dad: Tim, what did you learn in school today?

Tim: I learned to say, "Yes, sir," "No, sir," "Yes, Ma'am," and "No, Ma'am."

Dad: You did?

Tim: Yeah!

*   *   *

Caldwell had just returned from a long business trip. His son was proudly displaying all of the boy-scout merit badges he had recently received.

"How did you manage so many badges in so short a time?" asked Dad.

"Well," replied the boy, "my scoutmaster Mr. Dixon came over each night to advise me."

"So he worked with you?"

"Not really, Dad. Mom and Mr. Dixon would smile at each other, and then Mr. Dixon would give me a merit badge and advise me to take a hike."

* * *

"My," said Aunt Penelope, "you've put on some weight, haven't you?"

"I hope so," retorted Rob. "I weighed only eight pounds when I was born."

* * *

Osborne suggested to his ten-year-old boy that he ought to give up something for Lent—something that would really hurt, such as candy. The boy hesitated and finally asked what his father was giving up.

"Both your mother and I are giving up liquor," replied Osborne.

"But before dinner you were drinking something."

"Yes," acknowledged the father. "That was sherry. We gave up hard liquor."

"Okay, then, Dad, I think I'll give up hard candy."

*　　*　　*

Winston, a New York dentist in Las Vegas for a convention, took his eight-year-old son to one of the hotel shows. When it turned out that the topless girls were wearing only a snip or two of blue and gold the kid reacted with, "Wow! Wow! This is great!"

As Winston tried to figure out how to handle it, the boy gushed, "Look at that, Dad! They're wearing my school colors."

*　　*　　*

Willie was sitting at the breakfast table when his father barged into the kitchen and shouted. "Damn it!"

"What is the matter?" asked his mother.

"This brush is no good," said his father, "I can't shave with it."

"That's funny," said Willie. "It was okay this morning when I washed my bike with it."

*　　*　　*

"I am going to make a strawberry shortcake for dinner," said Mrs. Grant.

"Can I help?" asked her little girl.

"Sure," said the woman. "You can wash the strawberries."

Mrs. Grant gave her daughter a pan of strawberries. Soon she called, "Are you washing all the strawberries? Are you doing a good job?"

"Oh, yes, mother," said the youngster, "I'm using lots of soap!"

* * *

"Peter! Peter!"

"What, ma?"

"Are you spitting in the fish bowl?"

"No, ma, but I'm comin' pretty close."

* * *

Mother: Now, Jordan, don't you know you are not supposed to eat with your knife?

Jordan: I know, Mother, but my fork leaks!

* * *

"May I have another cookie?"

"Another cookie what?"

"Another cookie, please."

"Please who?"

"Please, Mother."

"Please, Mother what?"

"Please, Mother dear."

"Hell, no! You've had four already!"

* * *

Mary Sullivan, the super young-adult novelist, savors this smile getter:

Mrs. Kallin had been baking oatmeal cookies. While she had a batch in the oven, the phone rang in the den. After a long conversation, she remembered her cookies and rushed into the kitchen to find it filled with smoke.

Quickly she removed the charred cookie sheets and sat down utterly depressed. Suddenly, she felt the soft hand of her three-year-old. "Don't feel bad, Mama," said the tiny voice, "That's the best-smelling smoke you ever made."

Kenneth, a ten-year-old, was going to sell soda pop at the park, and asked his father to borrow a wrench.

"You mean a bottle opener, don't you?" suggested his father.

"No," said the boy, "a wrench. First I've got to turn off the water at all the drinking fountains."

* * *

Dinner's defrosting,
Mother's not;
Today's her birthday,
And Dad forgot.

* * *

Sweeney went to the family Thanksgiving dinner and found himself sitting beside a schoolboy nephew he had not seen for some time. "How old are you now?" he asked.

"How do you mean, exactly?" replied the youngster. "When I'm on a bus, when I go to the movies, or in real life?"

* * *

Mother: Another bite like that and you will have to leave the table.

Hungry Boy: Another bite like that and I'll be through.

70

Mrs. Anderson asked her son, "Why are you holding up that slice of bread?"

"I'd like to propose a toast!" said the boy.

*　　*　　*

"Be a good boy Lionel and eat your spinach," urged the boy's mother. "It will put color in your cheeks."

"But, ma," he whined, "who needs green cheeks?"

*　　*　　*

Grandma Ginsberg and her little grandson arrived early at Disneyland. For several hours they had a lot of fun, but it was an exhausting experience for Grandma. About noon, she decided to sit down and rest her aching feet. Realizing it was lunch time, she handed him some money.

"Here sonny. Take this and get somethin' to eat," she instructed. "But first, tell me what you're going to buy."

"Oh boy, three dollars!" exclaimed the youngster. "I'm gonna buy popcorn, peanuts, hot dogs, a candy apple, Cracker Jacks, ice cream . . . and . . . and . . ." He saw the old woman glaring at him and added, "and a green vegetable!"

*　　*　　*

"Evelyn, drink your milk like a good girl," ordered her mother. "It will make your teeth strong."

"Mama, if it's so good for the teeth," said the child taking a sip, "why don't you give my share to grandma?"

* * *

Cristabel had just turned seven, and for her birthday grandfather Dolan presented her with a doll.

"Mama, look at the lovely doll Gran'pa gave me!" she cried. "He's the best gran'pa in the world. When I grow up I'm going to marry him!"

"I'm afraid you can't do that, honey," said the mother. "You'd be marrying my father."

"But, Mommy," said the child, "you married mine!"

* * *

Sterling: Grandma, if I was invited out to dinner, should I eat pie with a fork?

Grandma: Yes, indeed, Sterling.

Sterling: You haven't got a pie in the house that I could practice on, have you Grandma?

* * *

GRANDMA

The baby sitter who does it for nothing.

* * *

Grandpa Davis looked very different to Shirley when he came on a recent visit. He had shaved off his big beard, and it was the first time she had seen him with a smooth, clean face.

"Oh, Grandpa!" exclaimed Shirley, "whose head have you got on?"

* * *

When Darren arrived at his grandmother's house in the country, she gave him permission to look at the lake nearby but not to go in the water.

An hour later, Darren showed up at the house with his long red hair drenched. Grandma demanded an explanation. "I fell in," explained Darren.

"Then how come your clothes are dry?" asked his grandparent.

"I took them off," replied the boy. "I had a feeling I was going to fall in."

* * *

Whitney's long-suffering parents deposited him at his grandmother's house for a two-week visit. The sweet old lady insisted that she was well able to handle the boy. The parents had their misgivings and were even more worried when they received his first letter:

Dear Mom and Pop,

It sure is nice here and we're having lots of fun. This morning me and Grandma played cops and robbers, and she's gonna bake me a whole bunch of cookies as soon as I untie her.

Love,
Whitney

*   *   *

It was Susan's first day at school and the experience proved too much for her. She returned home with her face down to the floor.

"What's the matter, honey?" her mother asked. "Didn't you like school?"

"No!" said Susan.

"Ah, I'll bet you were homesick," mother said.

"No," replied the child. "School sick."

*   *   *

Five-year-old Wendell rushed in from his weekly swimming lesson and excitedly told his grandmother that he'd taken a dive off the diving board.

"But you told me that last week," said his grandma.

"I know," said the boy, "But last week I was pushed."

*   *   *

Little Tommy: Grandpa, was you with Noah in the Ark?
Grandpa: I can't say I was.
Little Tommy: Then how come you wasn't drownded?

*   *   *

Mervin, age five, was giving his mother every conceivable argument why he should not go to school.

After telling him every reason why he should go to school, but without convincing him, his mother finally added, "Mervin, don't you know that if you didn't go to school your dad would have to go to jail?"

"For how long?" replied the boy.

*　　*　　*

Leila, aged six, was sent to visit her spinster aunt Imogene.

Leila's mother told her that Aunt Imogene was very prim and proper and that if she had to go to the bathroom Leila shouldn't say, "Auntie, I've got to go to the can!" She must say, "I've got to powder my nose!"

Leila arrived at her aunt's and for seven whole days she was a perfect lady. Whenever she had to go to the bathroom she said, "Excuse me, I've got to powder my nose!"

At the end of the week the spinster said, "I've just loved having you here. Next time you come please bring your little sister!"

"I don't think so, Auntie," said the child. "She's only three and she still powders her nose in bed!"

*　　*　　*

Mother: Why are you home from school so early?

Richard: I was the only one who could answer a question.

Mother: Oh! Really? What was the question?

Richard: Who threw the eraser at the principal?

*   *   *

BABY BAUBLES

Vernon, going on five, watched his mother put a clean diaper on his baby brother. When she didn't dust the infant with talcum powder, the boy shouted, "Wait, mother! You forgot to salt him."

* * *

One day, Bonnie's mother gave birth to twins. The next day, Bonnie's cat had six kittens. Her father kept the prettiest kitten and gave the rest away.

Bonnie went up to the twin's bassinet, pointed to one of the infants and announced, "I think this is the one we ought to get rid of!"

Mr. Cook had a baby girl
The stork left with a flutter;
Cook named her "Margarine,"
Cause he hadn't any but her.

* * *

One morning Annette went into her mother's bathroom and remarked on the size of her tummy.

"Well, dear, you see, daddy has given me a little baby."

The girl rushed into the bedroom and cried, "Daddy, did you give mummy a little baby?"

"Er . . . er . . . yes, I did," said the father.

"Well," said the daughter, "she's eaten it."

* * *

Monroe: What makes the new baby at your house cry so much?

Vaughn: It doesn't cry so very much. Besides, if all your teeth were out, your hair gone, and your legs so weak you couldn't stand on them, I guess you'd feel like crying yourself.

* * *

*   *   *

Fenton asked his mother where he came from.

"The stork brought you."

"And where did you come from?"

"Grandma found me under a cabbage leaf."

"And Grandma?"

"An angel slipped her into the doctor's little black bag."

"Mother," said Fenton, "do you mean to tell me there's been no sexual intercourse in our family for three generations?"

*   *   *

BABY

*An alimentary canal with
a loud voice at one end,
and no responsibility at
the other.*

*   *   *

Little Simon, on his first visit to the zoo, stared at the caged stork for a long while. Then he tugged at his father's sleeve and exclaimed, "Gee, Dad, he doesn't recognize me."

*   *   *

Martha Tolles, the top children's-book author, tells teens this titillator:

Teddy's mother was in the hospital so he went to visit her, and to see his new brother. The youngster wandered into a room across the hall which was occupied by a woman with a broken leg.

"Hello," he said. "How long have you been here?"

"Oh, about a month."

"Let me see your baby?" he then asked.

"I don't have a baby," replied the woman.

"Gee, you're slow," said Teddy. "My mama's here just two days and she's got one."

* * *

Why do older boys often offer to help with their baby brother's diapers?

It's a sure way to make a little change.

* * *

Mrs. Carlton was in her doctor's office for a routine checkup several weeks after the baby's birth. She brought Nicky, her five-year-old, with her.

The nurse held the new baby on her lap, cooed, and played with it, saying, "You must be quite proud of your new little sister, Nicky. I wish I had a baby like this."

"Well," said the boy, "why don't you stay home nights and get pregnant?"

* * *

Holden: Mother, was that policeman over there ever a little baby?
Mother: Why certainly. Of course.
Holden: Oh, I would just love to see a baby policeman!

* * *

After a great deal of controversy, a school adopted a sex-education program. Mrs. Brock hadn't been too enthusiastic about it and was worried about how her small daughter would react. One morning the youngster came home and said, "Mommy, guess what? We learned how to make babies today."

"What?" gasped her mother. Then calmly she asked, "Tell me, dear, how do you make babies?"

"Easy," said the little one, "You drop the y and add i-e-s."

*　　*　　*

What is the difference between a baby and a cow?

You give water to the cow and you get back milk.

*　　*　　*

Caroline was hired to babysit for young Rudy, and she was meeting him for the first time.

"Do you go to school?" she asked.

"Naw," said the little toughie, "I'm sent!"

*　　*　　*

Amanda Glazer, the future Beverly Hills socialite, regales girlfriends with this goodie:

Mrs. Carroll parked her infant in front of a bakery while she went inside to buy some rolls and bread. A few minutes later, an elderly dowager walked up to the carriage and chucking the child under the chin, cooed, "Whose itty bitty baby is ooo?"

The infant stared blankly at her. The senior citizen pinched his cheeks and persisted, "Whose little itsy bitsy kitsy witsy are you?"

Finally the kid kicked up his feet and snapped, "How the hell do you expect me to talk when I'm only three months old?"

*　　*　　*

Did you hear about the baby who was put in a higher bed—so that mama in the next room could hear if she fell out?

*　　*　　*

Eels in Spider Sauce! Oh, boy!
They're yummier than custard.
Tiny babies like them best,
With globs and globs of mustard.

*　　*　　*

Sophie, the babysitter, was pushing the baby carriage along a path in the park when a policeman strolled up.

"Fine-looking baby," he said. "How old is he?"

"He'll be a year old next week," answered Sophie.

"He doesn't look that old," said the policeman.

"No," replied the babysitter. "You see, he was very young when he was born."

*　　*　　*

    *   *   *

Baby stork to Mama stork: Well, at least give me a hint. Who *did* bring me?

    *   *   *

Halstead's parents decided not to tell him about the forthcoming of a small sister or brother. As time passed, it became more and more difficult to conceal the facts, and finally the boy was sent off to his grandfather's for a while.

Finally the blessed event happened. Halstead's Dad phoned Grandpa and asked him to break the news.

"My boy," said the grandfather, "you know that good old bird, the stork, had been flying pretty low over your house now for a while. Yes siree, he's been flying lower and lower, flapping his wings, circling down right over your house, and . . ."

"Gosh," said Halstead, "I hope he doesn't scare Mom. She's pregnant, you know."

    *   *   *

What's a good line for announcing the
birth of a baby daughter?
"We have skirted the issue."

*   *   *

SCHOOLHOUSE HIGHJINKS

Eight-year-old Lucas went to school one morning loaded down with a big bag of bubblegum which he passed out to his classmates. He even handed some to his surprised teacher, who asked, "What's this all about?"

"Oh," he said, "I just became a brother last night."

* * *

*   *   *

Teacher: Edmund, aside from a supersonic jet, what goes faster than the speed of sound?

Edmund: My Aunt Hyacinth when she talks.

*   *   *

Ten-year-old Wayne was asked by his teacher to name the four seasons of the year. His answer? "Football, basketball, baseball, and vacation!"

*   *   *

Miss Caldwell took her class to the San Diego zoo. When they passed the lion's cage, she asked, "What's the plural of lion?"

"Lions," answered Danny.

"What's the plural of sheep?" she asked.

"Sheep," replied Arlene.

"Right," said Miss Caldwell.

They soon came upon a hippopotamus. "What's the plural of hippopotamus?" the teacher asked Cameron.

"Who would want two of them?" answered the youngster.

*   *   *

*　　*　　*

The class was studying all about the people who work at airports. Miss Wells asked Jasper, "What do you call the person who tells the pilot where to land?"

"A hijacker!" said the little boy proudly.

*　　*　　*

For several months Boyce brought Miss Hanlon, his third-grade teacher, a bag of raisins. One day he came to class empty-handed. "Every morning for the past four months you've brought me a bag of raisins," said the teacher, "but today, you didn't. How come?"

"My rabbit died," replied the little boy.

*　　*　　*

"Sidney, if your father earned $350 a week and gave your mother half, what would she have?"

"Heart failure."

*　　*　　*

Little Davin began eating a frozen lemon popsicle just as the school bell rang, and since he didn't want to waste it, he stuck it in his pants' pocket.

In the classroom Miss Corwin asked Darlene what they called people who live at the North Pole.

"Eskimos," she replied.

Then teacher asked Loretta what they called people who live in Mexico.

She said, "Mexicans."

Miss Corwin asked Davin what they called people who live in Europe, and the youngster said, "I don't know."

Then super-smart Loretta shouted, "European."

And Davin said, "I am not—my popsicle is melting!"

Miss Lerman asked her class, "Who said, 'Give me liberty or give me death'?"

"Patrick Henry!" they all shouted.

Then she asked, "Can any of you tell me who said, 'I have come to bury Caesar, not to praise him'?"

Brad raised his hand and said, "The undertaker."

*   *   *

Ben, at school for the first time, began crying.

"What's the matter?" asked his teacher.

"I don't like school," he sobbed, "and I just found out I have to stay here till I'm 18."

"That's nothing," she replied. "I have to stay here till I'm 65."

*   *   *

Teacher: Now, boys, there is an important example to be learned from the life of the ant. Every day the ant goes to work and works all day. Every day the ant is busy. And in the end what happens?

Willard: Someone steps on him.

*   *   *

* * *

"If I cut two apples and two pears in ten pieces, what will I get?"

"Fruit salad."

* * *

Hilliard and Daphne, both eight years old, were walking home from school. He was carrying her books.

"Daphne," mooned Hilliard, "you are the first girl I have ever loved."

"Darn it," said Daphne, "I've drawn another beginner!"

* * *

One day in school young Calvin wrote on the blackboard, "Calvin is a passionate devil." The teacher reprimanded him for doing it and made him stay after school for one hour.

When he finally left the school that evening, all his playmates crowded about him, eager to hear what punishment he had received. "What did she do to you?" asked a friend.

"I ain't sayin' nothin'," replied Calvin, "except that it pays to advertise."

* * *

Teacher: Baldwin, what is a cannibal?
Baldwin: I don't know.
Teacher: Well, if you ate your father and mother, what would you be?
Baldwin: An orphan!

*   *   *

Dexter was kept in after school by his teacher. As he was walking home, a classmate approached him and asked, "What happened?"

"Nothing," he answered. "She's not my type."

*   *   *

Miss Witter had just finished reading the class a story about a man who swam a river three times before breakfast. Suddenly, she spotted Norman snickering.

"Don't you believe that a trained swimmer can do that?" she asked.

"Yes, ma'am," said Norman. "But I was just wondering why he didn't make it four times so he could get back to the side of the river where he left his clothes."

*   *   *

Little Sawyer came home from school and said to his mother, "Our teacher is really dumb. All four days this week she has asked us how much two and two is. We told her it was four. But she still doesn't know it; this morning she asked again."

*   *   *

Richie, age eight, came home and complained, "Ma, Teacher's picking on me again."

"Is that so?" said his mother angrily. "She's been picking on you all year. This has got to stop. Tomorrow, I'm going to school with you, and we'll have it out with her."

Next morning Richie and his mother arrived in the classroom and demanded an explanation from the teacher.

"I am not picking on your child," said the teacher. "I've never picked on any pupil. You might as well know the truth. Your son is not very bright, and when I say that, I'm being very kind. Let me show you what I mean.

"Richie," she called. "Tell us how much is five and five?"

"You see, Ma!" cried the boy, "she's picking on me again!"

*   *   *

Hillsborough's handsome Sterling Sidney Lanier III gets howls with this humdinger:

Goddard, the rural teacher, wanted to impress on his pupils the need to think before speaking. One morning he told them, "Count to 50 before saying anything important, and 100 if it is very important."

Next day, he was speaking, standing with his back to an electric heater, when he noticed several lips moving rapidly.

Suddenly the whole class shouted: ". . . 98, 99, 100. Your coat's on fire, sir!"

* * *

Did you hear about the schoolteacher who made her husband take her for a drive on a mountain road while she corrected papers?

She liked to grade on the curve.

* * *

Randall asked his teacher if a person should be punished for something he hadn't done.

"No," said the teacher. "Of course not."

"Good," said the little boy. "I haven't done my arithmetic."

* * *

"I did my good deed for today, Mom. I put a tack on the teacher's chair."

"You consider that a good deed?" said his horrified mother.

"Sure. Everybody in the class hates him."

* * *

*   *   *

"I won a prize in kindergarten today," boasted Edna to her mother. "Teacher asked me how many legs a hippopotamus has, and I said 'Three.' "

"Three?" asked her mother. "How on earth could you have won the prize?"

"I came the closest," said the little girl.

*   *   *

Teacher: Renaldo, if you put your hand in one pants' pocket and you find 30 cents, and you put your hand in the other pants' pocket and you find 70 cents, what would you have?

Renaldo: I'd have on somebody else's pants!

*   *   *

Miss Sutherland took her class on a tour of the White House, and then asked the students to write their impressions of the visit.

One boy wrote: *"I was especially glad to have this opportunity to visit my future home."*

*   *   *

Miss Thompson was irate. "This composition on 'Our Cat,' she exploded, "is word-for-word the same as your brother's."

"Yes, Ma'am," said Boyd, "it's the same cat."

*   *   *

Burt went to his uncle's garage and asked, "Could you lend me a few gallons of gas?"

"What do you need gas for?" asked the uncle.

"The school is burning."

*   *   *

Teacher: When is the right time to gather apples?
Herman: When the dog is chained up.

*   *   *

Here are two notes passed between a boy and a girl who sat next to each other in a third-grade class.

Wrote the boy: *"Dear Agnes: I luv you. Do you luv me? Mikey."*

Answered the girl: *"Dear Mikey: I do not love you. Love, Agnes."*

*   *   *

*   *   *

In a fourth-grade class the project for the month was to grow flowers and herbs from seeds.

Miss Davies asked the pupils whose mothers had plants at home. A number of hands went up.

Young Florence bounced out of her seat and called out, "I'm sure my mother can be a great help. She's always running off to meetings of Plant Parenthood!"

*   *   *

Here is a test question:
"Explain the manners and customs of the people of Borneo."
Here is the student's answer:
"The natives have no manners and they wear no costumes."

*   *   *

Teacher: How is the abbreviation "etc." used?

Jerome: To make people think we know more about something than we really do.

*   *   *

Miss Morgan used a ladder to write something up high on the blackboard for her sixth-grade class. In the front row, Alex Hall remarked, "Teacher, I can see up your skirt."

"That's a naughty thing to say, Alex. You're expelled for two days."

She reached up higher and Joey Demato said, "Teacher, I can see your thighs."

"Joey, you're expelled for a week."

Then the teacher reached way up. A moment later Leon Dumbrowski started walking toward the door. "Where are you going, Leon?" asked Miss Morgan.

"Well, teach," he replied, "I guess my school days are over."

* * *

"Name three collective nouns," asked Miss Haskell.

"Fly-paper, waste-basket, and vacuum-cleaner," answered wise Willie.

* * *

"Too bad you flunked the test," said Alicia. "How far were you from the right answer?"

"Two seats!"

* * *

*   *   *

English is tough to learn because we have a lot of words that can have more than one meaning.

A little immigrant boy from Viet Nam, now living in California, acquired a crush on his grade-school teacher. One bright morning he brought her a flower.

On the note that was attached to the flower, the well-meaning youngster had written this tender message:

"This little flower will fade and die but you, my dear teacher, will forever smell."

*   *   *

Miss Williams asked her hygiene class, "What is the function of the stomach?"

"To hold up your pants," answered a boy in the back row.

*   *   *

Juan walked into class almost 40 minutes late. "You should have been here at nine o'clock," said the teacher.

"Why? What happened?" asked the boy.

*   *   *

Susan Slater, the Los Angeles violin virtuoso, gets snickers with this snappy smiler:

Augusta and Brenda, both nine, were sitting beside each other.

"Don't you just hate this long bus ride to school every morning?" asked Augusta.

"Oh, I don't mind the bus ride," replied Brenda. "It's getting there that I don't like."

Miss Berkowitz had been having daily trouble with an unruly pupil, so she stopped by his Harlem home to speak with his parents.

The boy came to the door. She asked for his mother or father.

"They were here," he said, "but now they's gone."

"Where," she demanded, "is your grammar?"

"She's taking a nap," he said.

*   *   *

Teacher: What great event happened in 1809?
Malcolm: Abraham Lincoln was born.
Teacher: Correct. And what great event happened in 1812?
Malcolm: Abraham Lincoln had his third birthday.

*   *   *

Carmichael had to turn in an essay on Abraham Lincoln. Here is what he wrote:

"Abe Lincoln was born. Then he became a boy. Then he became a man. Then he became president. Then he was shot. The End."

*   *   *

*   *   *

Miss Selby was telling her third-grade class about children all over the world. When she got to Scotland she asked, "Can anybody tell me what lads and lassies are? Gabriel, I see your hand up. Tell the class."

"Lads," said Gabriel, "are boys, and lassies are dogs."

*   *   *

Miss Dunhill had asked her pupils to name the nine greatest Americans. All the students had turned in their papers except Stewart.

"Can't you finish your list, Stewart?"

"Not yet," replied the boy. "I'm still undecided about the third baseman."

*   *   *

Quenton finished his breakfast, then rushed off to school without washing his face.

His teacher looked at him and said, "You didn't wash your face. What would you say if I came to school with egg and jam all over my face?"

"Nothing," replied the boy. "I'd be too polite."

*   *   *

*   *   *

"What are the three words most often used by students?"

"I don't know."

"That's correct."

*   *   *

Exasperated Teacher: I asked all of the dumbbells to stand and you're the only one who did, Humphrey. Are you a dumbbell?

Humphrey: No, but I thought you might be a little lonely standing there all by yourself.

*   *   *

"No, I don't get the best marks in school, Daddy. Do you get the best salary at your office?"

*   *   *

Did you hear about the little girl who asked the gift-card salesman, "Got anything in blank report cards?"

*   *   *

Miss Dorsey stood up before her class and said, "Give me a sentence with a direct object."

"Teacher," said Kirk from the rear, "everybody thinks you're beautiful."

"Why, thank you, but what is the object?"

"A good report card," said the boy.

*   *   *

SCENE IN A NEW YORK CITY SCHOOL

Teacher: Louis, use these words in a sentence—defense, detail, deduct, defeat.

Louis: De-feat of de-duct went over defense before de-tail.

*   *   *

In a Queens grammar school the English teacher asked Anthony, "Compose a sentence in which the word 'torture' is used."

"Well," said Anthony, thinking hard, "just as the guy jumped onto the fire escape he turned to the lady and said, 'I torture husband was in Trenton.' "

*   *   *

"Here is my report card, Daddy, and one of yours I found in the attic."

*　　*　　*

Theobald walked into the living room and spoke to his father. "Pop," he said enthusiastically. "I've got great news for you."

The father smiled and asked, "What is it?"

"Remember you promised me $5 if I passed in school?"

The father nodded.

"Well," said the son, "I'm sparing you that expense this year."

*　　*　　*

A teacher called for sentences using the word "beans."

"My father grows beans," said the bright boy of the class.

"My mother cooks beans," said another girl.

Then a third popped up, "We're all human beans."

*　　*　　*

During the 1950's, the Principal of a midwest public school began collecting the answers kids wrote to test questions. He put them in a safety-deposit box and wrote in

116

his will that they were to be opened and read in the 1980's—only when *those kids* had become parents. Here are a few of the best . . . maybe some written by your mom and pop.

Etiquette is little things you do that you don't want to do.

A skeleton is a man or person without meat or skin.

An illiterate child is one whose parents are not married.

The wife of Columbus was Columbine.

If the baby doesn't thrive on fresh milk, it should be boiled.

We lost our dog. He was our pest for the past seven years.

An outlaw is a person who kicks his in-law out.

A prune is a plum that didn't take care of itself.

A baby whale is called a sardine.

To keep milk from turning sour, keep it in the cow.

When roasting lamb, my mother puts her leg in the oven.

And the dog jumped across the water in two jumps.

LITTLE SQUIRT SMILES

Five-year-old Jeff came home from his first day at kindergarten.

"How big is your class?" asked his mother.

"Ah!" he said disgustedly, "Four other fellows, and about a half-a-million girls!"

* * *

* * *

Marilyn, age six, went home and told her mom she was in love with a boy in her class and was going to marry him.

"That's nice," said her mother, going along with the gag. "Does he have a job?"

"Oh, yes," said Marilyn, "He erases the blackboard in our class."

* * *

Doting Mother: And what did mama's little darling learn at school today?

Sonny: I learned two punks not to call me mama's little darling.

* * *

Victor came home from his first day at school and told his mother he was never going back.

"What's the use of school?" he said. "I can't read and I can't write, and the teacher won't let me talk."

* * *

*   *   *

Kandy, in the first grade, admitted to her parents that she had been kissed that day in school by Mr. Armand Kajian.

"Is Armand in your class?" asked her amused father.

"No, he's an older man," admitted Kandy. "He's in the second grade."

*   *   *

Mrs. Higby wanted to enter her child in a modern kindergarten, but the child was only four, and the age requirement was five. "I think," said the mother, "that she can pass the five-year-old test."

"We shall see," said the teacher. Then to the child she said, "Dear, just say a few words that come into your mind."

"Mother," said the four-year-old, "does the lady want logically-connected sentences or merely irrelevant words?"

*   *   *

"Is ink so very expensive, father?"

"Why, no, what makes you think so?"

"Well, mother seems quite disturbed because I spilled some on the hall carpet."

*   *   *

*   *   *

Steven was in a Beverly Hills store with his mother, when he was given a stick of candy by one of the clerks.

"What do you say, Steven?" said his mother.

"Charge it!" he replied.

*   *   *

Arthur: Today on the school bus a little
            boy fell off his seat, and everybody
            laughed except me.
Teacher: Who was the little boy?
Arthur: Me.

*   *   *

Miss Stern read several familiar nursery rhymes to her little charges and then said, "Now, who can remember any of these and wants to stand up and recite?"

Karen raised her hand and said, "I know *Little Miss Muffet*."

"Good," said the teacher. "Let's hear it."

Karen stood up and recited proudly, " 'Little Miss Muffet sat on a tuffet, eating her curves away.' "

*   *   *

*   *   *

Accompanying her mother to a Seattle shoe shop, a little girl asked innocently, "When will I be old enough to wear shoes that are too small for me?"

*   *   *

The elevator operator at Gimbel's said to a little girl holding her mother's hand, "You must want the toy department."

"No, thanks," said the child. "We just came in to use the bathroom."

*   *   *

Returning after a lengthy absence to his family's spot on the beach, Jaimie found them getting ready to leave.

"Come along," said his mother. "We're going to a restaurant for dinner."

"I'm not hungry," was the reply. "I've eaten five ice cream cones and eight hot dogs with mustard and relish."

"Where on earth did you get them?" his mother asked. "You didn't have any money."

"I didn't need money. I just wandered all around the beach crying and making believe I was lost!"

*   *   *

Beverly Aucoin, the Los Angeles Super-Exec Sec, tells this tidbit for large tickles:

Farley, age six, watched his father change from a business suit to his tuxedo. Suddenly, the boy began crying.

"What's the matter?" asked his father.

"Daddy, please don't wear that suit. It always gives you such a headache the next morning!"

Grandma was babysitting Wilbur. She asked, "Would you like to go to the carnival and ride the merry-go-round?"

"I don't mind, if it will amuse you," answered the boy.

*   *   *

Ellen: I wish I had been born a hundred years ago.
Mother: My goodness, why?
Ellen: You wouldn't dare ask a little old lady to make her own bed.

*   *   *

Four-year-old Lois was showing the family's new bathroom scale to five-year-old Eric.

"What is it?" asked Eric.

"I don't know, but when Mommy and Daddy stand on it, it makes them mad."

*   *   *

Dennis was a bad boy, so his mother decided to punish him. "Dennis," she cried, "go find a strap and bring it to me."

Dennis returned in a few minutes. "I couldn't find a strap, Mother," he said, "but here are some rocks you can throw at me."

* * *

Taken to the dentist for a checkup, Duncan was told he'd have to have a filling.

"Now, Duncan," asked the dentist, "what kind of filling would you like for that tooth?"

"Chocolate, please," replied the youngster.

* * *

A small boy was walking along, crying bitterly. "What's the trouble, son?" asked a kindly gentleman.

"My mother lost her psychology book," explained the lad between sobs, "and now she's using her own judgment."

* * *

Marc: Say, Dad, that apple I just ate had a worm in it, and I ate that too.
Dad: Wait! Here, drink this water and wash it down.
Marc: Nah, let him walk down!

* * *

"What do you want to be when you grow up?"
"Alive!"

* * *

Mrs. Harrison's seven-year-old daughter came home from camp sporting a gold medal for packing her trunk more neatly than any other girl.

"How did you do it," marveled her mother, "when at home you can never clean up the mess you leave behind?"

"It was a cinch," explained the girl. "I just never unpacked it all summer."

* * *

Donald's mother sent him to a progressive camp. One Sunday she arrived for a visit and found he was quite excited about having gone swimming in the camp pool.

"But how did you do that?" she asked. "I forgot to pack your bathing trunks for you."

"I went in naked."

"Did the girls go in naked, too?"

"Oh, no," he replied, "they wore bathing caps."

* * *

Little Josh, seized with hiccups, cried, "Mommy, I'm coughing backward."

* * *

* * *

Vic's mother told him, "You mustn't pull the cat's tail like that."

"I'm only holding it, Mom," he said. "The cat is pulling."

* * *

Asked why he always gobbled his food, a nine-year-old explained: "It tastes so good that I want to eat all I can before I lose my appetite."

* * *

Dolores, a first-grader, informed her mother that she had broken her engagement to a classmate.

"What's the matter?" asked her mother.

"He just isn't ready for marriage yet," she explained. "And besides, he scribbled in my coloring book."

* * *

"Why did you kick your little brother in the stomach?"

"He turned around."

* * *

Melissa, age six, invited Naomi, a playmate, to spend the night with her. Next morning, seeking mischief, they tiptoed into the parents' bedroom. Naomi went to the dresser to look at a picture of Melissa's father taken when he was in college.

"Who's that?" whispered Naomi.

"That's my daddy," replied Melissa.

Naomi looked at Melissa's father asleep in bed and then asked, "Then who is that man in bed with your mommy?"

*　　*　　*

Tiny Priscilla waiting to be vaccinated was determined to be brave. Everything went okay until she was face-to-face with the needle.

She leaned over and spoke softly into the doctor's ear, "I think your mother is calling you."

*　　*　　*

Matthew was getting his third polio shot.

"Which arm would you like it in?" asked the doctor.

"Mother's!" replied the boy.

*　　*　　*

Ralph had a cold so the doctor came to see him. "Let me look in your ears," the medico said.

Ralph let him look.

"Now open your mouth."

Ralph opened his mouth.

"Now stick out your tongue," said the doctor.

"Why?" asked Ralph. "I'm not mad at you!"

*　　*　　*

Six-year-old: I wonder what thumbs are for?

Four-year-old: They're to hold up bottoms of sandwiches.

*   *   *

Mrs. Sandberg was shocked to hear the language used by her little daughter Mia. When asked, Mia said she had learned it from a girl she played with in the park.

The next day Mrs. Nelson found her daughter's playmate in the park.

"Are you the little girl who uses bad words?"

"Who told you?"

"A little bird," answered the woman.

"Well, I like that!" exclaimed the small girl. "And I've been feeding the little bastards, too!"

*   *   *

Neighbor: Does your new baby brother cry much, Gerald?

Gerald: He cries when you stick pins in him or make faces at him or bounce him up and down. But what can you expect? He's too little to swear.

*   *   *

* * *

"What's all that racket you're making in the pantry, Son?"

"I'm fighting temptation, Mom."

* * *

Pete and Norman were playing marbles together when a very pretty little girl walked by.

Pete stopped and said to his pal, "Boy, when I stop hating girls, she's the one I'm going to stop hating first!"

* * *

Alan's dog was run over and he mourned for days and days. "Oh come now, Alan," said his father. "You didn't carry on this way when grandma died."

"Yeah," cried Alan, "but I didn't raise grandma from a pup."

* * *

Eleanor refused some food at the table, and snapped, "I don't like it."

"Don't say that," chirped her younger brother. "The more you don't like a thing the gooder it is for you."

* * *

* * *

"Sorry you have a toothache. I'd have that tooth pulled if it were mine."

"So would I, if it was yours."

* * *

Visitor: And what are you going to do when you grow up dear?

Jessica: I'm going to raise mint.

Visitor: Mint?

Jessica: Yes, that's where Daddy says all our money comes from.

* * *

Stanley and Martin, two brothers, wanted to ask a favor of their mother.

"You ask her," said Stanley, age eleven.

"No," said Martin, age ten. "You ask her. You've known her longer than I have."

* * *

"Are you a little boy or a little girl?"

"Sure, what else could I be?"

* * *

*   *   *

Edgar was about to have his tonsils out and said, "I'll be a good boy, mommy, but I don't want a crying baby like they gave you at the hospital. I want a puppy!"

*   *   *

Little Joe, four, sat next to a man eating Limburger cheese. When he couldn't stand the odor any longer he said, "Wow—I wish my nose was deaf and dumb!"

*   *   *

Beatrice wanted to be a doctor when she grew up. She bandaged and cared for her dolls, and often would go on imaginary sick calls to someone in the neighborhood.

One day she ran out on such a mercy errand, forgetting to close the door behind her. When her mother insisted she come back and shut it, Beatrice did so and raced away.

That evening her mother asked, "How is the patient getting along?"

"She died," said the girl. "Died while I was closing that darn door."

*   *   *

One evening Philip's father brought his boss home for dinner. When Philip's mother served the meat, the little boy asked, "Is this mutton?"

"No," replied his mother. "Why do you ask?"

"Because Dad said he was going to bring some muttonhead home for dinner," answered Philip.

* * *

"Where was your big brother going with that bag of oats?"

"Taking his girl out to dinner. He says she eats like a horse."

* * *

At bedtime Mother was telling Lucas of when she was a little girl. The boy listened excitedly as Mom told of having a Shetland pony and a cart, going to a country fair, and swimming in the stream near the farm.

Finally he sighed, "Gee, Mama, I wish I had met you earlier."

* * *

Mother: What do you want to take your cod-liver oil with this morning, Basil?

Basil: A fork!

Adrienne Jones, the jovial juvenile novelist, gets big jollies with this younger-generation jest:

One August day, seven-year-old Norma was walking down the street carefully leading her younger brother, Ted. The little boy had his eyes tightly closed.

A senior citizen stopped them and asked, "What's the matter? Has he hurt his eyes?"

"Oh, no," answered Norma, "We do this every Saturday when the sun's so bright. He keeps his eyes closed and I lead him to the movies. When we're inside, he opens his eyes and finds us both a seat."

Marjorie said to her playmate, "I have to leave now, Mama's giving a party and I gotta go home and say bright things for the company."

*　　*　　*

Mother: No, Eddie, you must not be selfish. You must let your little brother have the sled half the time.

Eddie: But, Mother, I do. I have it going down the hill, and he has it coming up.

*　　*　　*

"Dad, give me a quarter."

"Not today, Son, not today."

"Dad, if you give me a quarter, I'll tell you what the milkman said to mama this morning."

"Here, Son, quick—what did he say?"

"He said, 'Lady, how much milk do you want this morning?' "

*　　*　　*

"William, stop poking the baby."

"I'm not poking him, Ma, I'm counting his measles."

*　　*　　*

Steve came running into the kitchen yelling, "Mama, there's the funniest man in front of our house."

His mother said, "Is that so, what is he doing?"

"Well," said the boy, "he's just sitting on the sidewalk and yelling at a banana peel I left there!"

*   *   *

Benjy came home with a bloody nose and his mother asked him what happened.

"A kid bit me," he cried.

"Would you recognize him if you saw him again?" asked his mom.

"Sure," sniffed the little boy. "I'd know him anywhere. I've got his ear in my pocket."

*   *   *

"Why is your little brother crying?"

"He just came down the stairs without walking."

*   *   *

"I never told lies when I was a child."

"When did you begin, mother?"

*   *   *

141

Mother: Aunt Mathilda won't kiss you with that dirty face.

Archie: That's what I figured.

* * *

Connie, age six, asked, "Mommy, what does physical attraction mean?"

"You have plenty of time to think about that," answered her mother. "When you're old enough you'll meet the right man. Together you'll have mutual interests like sports, literature, music, and so on. To you, he will be handsome, considerate, and kind. Do you understand?"

"I think so, Mommy," replied Connie. "But tell me, is that better than sex?"

BIBLICAL BEAUTS

Georgie was overheard saying his prayers: "Please, God, make Paris the capital of Italy."

"But, Georgie," asked his mother, "why ask for that?"

"Because that's what I put on my test papers in school today."

* * *

*　　*　　*

Miss Mattson smiled at her Sunday-School group and exclaimed, "All right, class, all those who want to go to heaven raise your hands."

Everybody in the class had a hand raised, except Wally. "Don't you want to go to heaven?" asked the teacher.

"I can't, ma'am. My mom wants me to come straight home."

*　　*　　*

California vacationers Amber and Shana Angel crack-up over this nifty nugget:

Miss Walsh, the Sunday-School teacher, asked her class on Easter morning, "Can any of you tell us what we celebrate on Easter?"

"I can," spoke up little Tess, waving her hand eagerly. "We celebrate Christ coming out of the tomb."

"That's correct," cried the teacher. "It's wonderful that one so young should know that!"

"Yes," continued the tyke, "and if he sees his shadow, he goes back in for another six weeks."

*　　*　　*

*   *   *

The following are some biblical questions with answers by smart kids that have turned Sunday School teachers topsy-turvy:

Teacher: Who can tell us something about Good Friday?

Jimmy: He was the fellow who helped Robinson Crusoe.

*   *   *

What evidence is there in the Bible that Adam and Eve were noisy?
They raised Cain.

*   *   *

If you throw a blue stone into the Red Sea, what will it become?
Wet.

What did Adam first plant in the Garden of Eden?
His foot.

When was the first time walking sticks popped up in the Bible?
When Eve presented Adam with a little Cain.

What's the purpose of a cocktail called "The Ark"?

It's for the people who can't say Noah.

Who didn't hang up his clothes when he went to bed?

Adam.

Who was the first man mentioned in the Bible?

Chap. One.

Who was the first girl mentioned in the Bible?

Gene-sis.

Who was the straightest man in the Bible?

Joseph, because Pharoah made a ruler out of him.

Why didn't they play cards on the Ark?

Because Noah was sitting on the deck.

Who was the most successful doctor in the Bible?

Job, because he had the most patients.

Why is a pair of skates like an apple?

Because both are responsible for the fall of man.

What was the cause of Adam's first real argument with Eve?

He caught her putting his best Sunday suit into the salad.

At what time did God create Adam?
A little before Eve.

How were Adam and Eve prevented from gambling?

Their pair o'dice was taken away from them.

Why didn't the ancients use slates and pencils?

Because the Lord told them to multiply on the face of the earth.

What did Noah say when the animals started climbing into the Ark?

"Now I herd everything!"

What animals failed to come to Noah's Ark in pairs?

Worms. They came in apples.

Where did Noah keep his bees?
In the Ark hives.

Who is the most popular actor in the Bible?

Samson—he brought the house down.

How did Jonah feel when the whale swallowed him?

Down in the mouth.

Who killed a fourth part of all the people in the world?

Cain, when he killed Abel.

When was paper money first mentioned in the Bible?

When the dove brought green back to Noah.

Where was Solomon's Temple?

On the side of his head.

What is a minister doing when he rehearses his sermon?

Practicing what he preaches.

* * *

Little Vernon asked the preacher,

"When are you going to preach against floating kidneys?"

"What do you mean?" the preacher asked.

"Well, last Sunday you talked about loose livers."

* * *

*   *   *

What's the difference between Noah's Ark and Joan of Arc?

One was made of wood, the other was Maid of Orleans.

*   *   *

After Sunday School Miss Harper stopped to chat with Neville:

Teacher: What did you do when Kyle called you a liar?
Neville: I remembered what you told me: "A soft answer turns away wrath."
Teacher: Very good, Billy. What answer did you give him?
Neville: I answered him with a soft tomato.

*   *   *

José came home after his first day in Sunday School and told his mother that the teacher asked him where he was born.

"You said the hospital, didn't you?" asked his mother.

"Nah. I didn't wanna sound like a sissy so I said Dodger Stadium."

*   *   *

Ira Perlman, the Long Island auto-parts mogul, loves this little lulu:

Karen, age six, had been praying every night for weeks, asking God to please send her a baby sister. One day she was taken to her mother's room to see her twin sisters. The little girl was delighted. That night, she prayed like this:

"Dear God, thank You for sending me a baby sister, but I thought You would like to know that she arrived in two pieces."

*　　*　　*

A five-year-old was sent to Sunday school with this note pinned to her coat: *"The opinions expressed by this child concerning God and the Bible may not be necessarily those of her family."*

*　　*　　*

"What would you do if you saw Jesus in the street?"

"Go up to him, give him a Bible and say, 'This is Your Life'!"

*　　*　　*

Julius came home from Bible class one Sunday, and confronted his parents with the surprising news that Biblical children used profanity. "Even babies swore," asserted the boy.

"That's not true," said his mother. "Little boys and girls never used dirty words, and it doesn't say so in the Bible either. As far as babies cursing in Old Testament days, that's ridiculous!"

"But, Mother," argued Julius. "I read it myself, this morning. It says that Job cursed the day he was born!"

*　　*　　*

Teacher: What did the three wise men bring
the Christ child?

Pupil: Gold, Frankenstein, and mermaids.

*   *   *

There was a young lady in Guam
Who said, "Now the ocean's so calm,
    I will swim for a lark."
    She encountered a shark.
Let us now sing the Ninety-Third psalm.

*   *   *

Robbie walked into the kitchen and
tugged on his mother's apron.

"What is it, dear?" she inquired.

"Is it true that we come from dust and
we return to dust?"

"Yes, darling. That's what the Bible
says."

"Well," retorted Robbie, "I just looked
under my bed and somebody's either coming or going!"

*   *   *

Cathy was kneeling down and saying
her prayers. Suddenly her four-year-old
brother sneaked up behind her and pulled
her hair. "Pardon me, God," said Cathy.
"I'll be right back after I boot Barney in the
butt!"

*   *   *

Audrey refused to say her prayers and it was causing her parents great concern.

"You should thank the Lord for everything you have," said her mother.

"Why?" asked the child.

"There are millions of children who would love to have good food, a lovely room, pretty clothes, doting parents. . . . Just think how miserable they must be."

"If that's true," said Audrey, "then they're the ones who need to say their prayers."

*   *   *

Margot, age six, was sent up to bed after dinner. "Say good-night to all our guests," said her mother, "and don't forget to say your prayers."

"Okay," said the child. "Anybody need anything?"

*   *   *

After an hour of trying, Mitchel finally got his kite launched. Then all of a sudden the wind died down.

"Oh, please, God," said he to the heavens, "no matter what you do, don't stop breathing now."

*   *   *

Gwendolyn was the source of much distress to her parents. The little girl exaggerated and distorted everything out of proportion.

She was offered a cute puppy for her sixth birthday, provided that she stop telling tall tales. The child agreed. But soon Gwendolyn went about the neighborhood informing the other children that she had been given a lion.

"Young lady," said her mother, "you march right upstairs and ask God to forgive you for telling a falsehood. A lion indeed!"

Meekly, the little girl went upstairs, but soon returned wearing an angelic smile on her face.

"Did you ask God to forgive you?" asked the mother.

"Yes, mama," replied Gwendolyn, "but He told me not to worry about it. He can hardly tell the difference Himself!"

* * *

Uncle Bob: Were you a polite little boy in church this morning?

Frankie: Yeah. A man held out a big plate full of money, and I said, "No, thank you."

* * *

Norm Woodard, Washington's book-service wizzard, gets yucks with this whimsical winner:

Felix was saying his prayers while his daddy listened and waited to kiss his son good-night.

After the usual, *"Now I Lay Me Down to Sleep,"* the youngster bestowed blessings on each member of the family, various neighbors, friends, the family cat, dog, and goldfish.

Just as he was about to conclude, he blurted out, "Oh, one more thing. Dear God, please give some money to those poor ladies in my daddy's magazines, so they can buy some clothes!"

Dorothy was thrilled when she received the two gifts she had most wanted: a wristwatch with a tiny alarm bell, and a vial of perfume. She chattered about her new possessions all day long, wearying her parents with the subject.

That night Father Callahan, from Saint Patrick's Church, was expected for dinner.

"Dorothy, everybody knows about your watch with the bell, and the perfume, too," said her mother. "But, you mustn't talk about them all the time—especially in front of our parish priest."

At dinner, the child kept quiet through most of the meal, barely able to hold back her exciting news. Finally, unable to control herself, she tapped the priest on the arm.

"Father," she cried, "if anyone hears anything or smells anything, it's me!"

TEEN TITTERS

Metcalf, a Chicago bus driver, kept harassing his son about what he wanted to be when he grew up.

After being pestered to death, the son finally answered, "I want to be a bus driver, until I get a job."

* * *

Roberta: My ancestors came over on the Mayflower.
Hayward: It's lucky for them. Immigration laws are stricter now.

* * *

"Why don't you get out and find a job?" a gruff father said to his son. "When I was your age I was working for $10 a week in a store. After five years, I owned it."

"You can't do that nowadays," said the boy. "They have cash registers."

*   *   *

It's done beneath the mistletoe,
It's done beneath the rose.
But the proper place to kiss, you know,
Is just beneath the nose.

*   *   *

Heather and Kelly, two teenagers, were chatting over cokes.

"My older sister has spent her whole life chasing men," said Heather.

"Did she ever catch one?" asked Kelly.

"No, but she's personally responsible for several men qualifying for the Olympic track team."

*   *   *

"They do say," Scott began shyly, "that kisses are the language of love."

"Well, speak up."

*   *   *

A thirteen-year-old girl had this list of babysitting prices:

Sleeping babies—$2
Crying babies—$3
Wet babies—$4
Worse than wet babies—$5

*   *   *

Ryan, age sixteen, turned in to the family driveway at the wheel of the family car. His father sat beside him. Several younger brothers came out to meet them.

"I just passed my driving test!" shouted Ryan proudly. "You guys all move up one bike."

*   *   *

"Did you hear the news? My rich uncle fell off a cliff."

"Were you very close to him?"

"Just close enough to push."

*   *   *

Rupert and Dexter were chatting during football practice:

"Wendy sure is a smart girl," remarked Rupert. "She has brains enough for two."

"Then she's just the girl for you," said Dexter.

Linc Klemola, the Hanna, Wyoming bait-and-tackle king, coddles customers with this cute bit of kidding:

Nicole wanted to be alone with Jason but little brother kept hanging around.

"He's not very s-m-a-r-t," spelled Nicole.

"No," agreed Jason. "He looks like a little d-o-p-e for a twelve-year-old."

"It's okay with me if you wanna go to the movies," said little brother. "You don't have to spell it."

Daddy bought a little car,
And feeds it gasoline.
And everywhere that Daddy goes
He walks—his son's sixteen.

*   *   *

"My girl often compares me with Robert Redford," said the sophomore.

"But there's no comparison," replied his pal.

"Yeah, that's what my girl says."

*   *   *

Rick: What's the best way to teach a girl to swim?

Mike: That requires technique. First you put your left arm around her waist. Then you gently take her left hand and . . .

Rick: She's my sister.

Mike: Oh, push her off the dock!

*   *   *

"Oh, Horace, honey, you say the cutest, sweetest things. You know, I don't think I ever really appreciated you till you got this new red sports car. It's changed your whole personality."

*   *   *

164

*   *   *

PEDESTRIAN

*The father of a teenager who didn't
think the family needed two cars.*

*   *   *

In Physics class Mr. Chapin was talking about displacement. "Miss Beck," he said, "would you be good enough to tell the class what happens when a body is placed in water?"

"Certainly," said the most popular girl in the school. "The telephone rings."

*   *   *

Son: Dad, the Bible says if you don't let me have the car, you hate me.
Dad: Where does it say that?
Son: Proverb 16:12. *"He that spareth the rod hateth his son."*

*   *   *

"Oh, mother, may I go out to swim?"
"Why not, my darling daughter.
You're so damned near naked anyhow,
You'd look better in the water."

*   *   *

"Do you love me, Derek?" whispered Linda.

"Of course I do," said the boy. "But, listen, my name is Maurice."

"Oh, that's right," said the girl. "I keep thinking this is Saturday."

* * *

"My old car is just like a little baby."

"Why's that?"

"It never goes anywhere without a rattle."

* * *

Jennifer was given a beautiful charm bracelet for her birthday. She wore it to school, but nobody noticed it. Finally she stood up and said, "My, it's so hot in here. I think I'll take off my bracelet."

* * *

Sherry and Jack were sitting in her living room.

"Sometimes my father takes things apart to see why they don't go."

"So?" asked the boy.

"So, you'd better go."

* * *

Harold, the school nitwit, approached Cassie, the prettiest cheerleader.

"I bet you wouldn't go out with me in a million years," he said.

"That's not true," replied the school beauty.

"You mean you might go out with me?"

"Sure," said Cassie. "Call me in a million years."

* * *

Gil: I thought your girl's name was Ogden.

Woody: It is.

Gil: How come you call her the Gillette girl?

Woody: Haven't you listened to her? She's always saying "Gillette me have a coke, Gillette me have a malt, Gillette me have a hot fudge. . . ."

* * *

A young lady, announcing plans to marry her childhood sweetheart, was asked if her parents had given their consent.

"Not yet," she said. "Father hasn't expressed his opinion yet, and Mother is waiting to contradict him."

* * *

A man who used to drop the boy off at school on his way to work. Now, he has a boy who drops him off at work on his way to school.

* * *

Bernadette, 16, and Marshall, 17, were about to be married. Their parents were opposed to the wedding, but nevertheless stood by as the minister conducted the service.

Reverend Carnwell asked the youthful bridegroom to repeat after him, "With all my worldly goods, I thee endow."

Marshall's mother nudged his father and whispered, "There goes his bike."

NUTTY NIFTIES

The man was drowning. "Help, I can't swim," he cried. "I can't swim!"

"I can't either," said an old man, sitting on the riverbank fishing. "But I'm not hollerin' about it."

*　　*　　*

"Ask me if I'm a rabbit."

"Okay, are you a rabbit?"

"Yes, I'm a rabbit. Now ask me if I'm an alligator."

"I'm game. Are you an alligator?"

"No, you loon. I told you I'm a rabbit."

*   *   *

The department-store Santa Claus was interviewing Kipp:

Santa: How old are you, little boy?

Kipp: Five years old.

Santa: What does your father do?

Kipp: He works at Tarbide and Tarbon Temical Tompany.

Santa: What do they make there?

Kipp: Light bulbs and toilet paper.

Santa: What makes you think that?

Kipp: That's what daddy always brings home in his lunch bucket!

*   *   *

"What's the matter, little boy? Why are you crying?"

"My mother went and drowned all the kittens."

"Ahh, that's too bad."

"Yeah," he cried, "She promised me I could do it."

*   *   *

Hugo and Jason were bragging about the accomplishments of their fathers.

"My old man was the first man to fly 10,000 feet with a stick in his hand," boasted Hugo.

"Oh, he was a flyer?" asked Jason.

"No. The poolroom blew up."

170

*   *   *

Harold, Ritchie and Millard were boasting about their fathers.

"My father bathes twice a week," said Harold.

"That's nothing," said Ritchie. "My father bathes three times a week."

"Oh, yeah?" said Millard, "My old man keeps himself so clean he never has to take a bath."

*   *   *

"Grandpa won't live much longer. You might say he has one foot in the grate."

"Don't you mean one foot in the grave?"

"No—he wants to be cremated."

*   *   *

Jay and Felix were playing cowboys. They brought their imaginary steeds to a halt before the empty grapefruit crate, serving as the Sidewinders Saloon. Jay swaggered up, pounded on the bar, and growled, "I'll have rye."

Felix, who was much younger, imitated Jay's swagger, and piped out from under an oversized hat, "And I'll have whole wheat."

*   *   *

171

Glendale's gleeful B. G. Willison gets guffaws with this goony giggler:

For his eighth birthday, Delwin received a brand new bicycle, with strict warnings that he ride it only with extra care. Reynolds, a neighbor, found him at the corner a few mornings later, staring at the bike's chain which had come off the sprocket.

Reynolds made the necessary repairs, smearing his new suit with mud in the process. "There you are, Delwin," he announced. "Now that you're eight, you'll soon be able to fix loose chains like that yourself."

"Heck," said Delwin, "I can do it faster than you can now—but I don't like to get my hands dirty."

Hershel was sent by his mother to buy an 85-cent loaf of rye at Berman's Bakery. While Berman was putting the bread into a bag, the boy noticed that the loaf was not very large.

"Isn't that a small loaf of bread for 85 cents?" he asked.

"You'll have less to carry," said the baker.

Hershel put 50 cents on the counter.

"You are 35 cents short," said Berman.

"That's right," replied the boy. "You'll have less to count."

*   *   *

Little Louis looked downcast and sad as he stood in front of Beauford the bus driver, searching in all his pockets for his money.

"What's the matter, son?" asked Beauford.

"I've lost the quarter that my mother gave me for bus fare to town and back," said Louis.

The bus driver was taken by the little boy's sad plight and gave him a free bus token.

"Thank you," said the boy, "but what about my change?"

*   *   *

Walter: I bet I can make you say "black."
What are the colors of the flag?

Mother: Red, white, and blue.

Walter: I told you that I could make you say "black."

Mother: I didn't say black.

*   *   *

Harlow telephoned the dentist's office and said, "I'm supposed to make an appointment."

"I'm sorry," said the nurse, "but the dentist is out of town."

"Thank you," said the boy. "When will he be out of town again?"

*   *   *

Greg and Paul were making sand castles at an Atlantic City beach.

"I'm really worried," said little Greg. "Dad slaves away at his job, so I'll never want for anything, and so I can go to college. Mom spends every day washing and ironing, cleaning up after me, and taking care of me when I get sick. I'm worried."

"What have you got to worry about?" asked Paul.

"I'm afraid they might try to escape."

*   *   *

* * *

The fourth grader was in bed with a cold and a high temperature.

"How high is it, Doctor?" he wanted to know.

"A hundred-and-three, son," said the doctor.

"What's the world's record?"

* * *

Old Mother Hubbard
Went to the cupboard,
To get her poor daughter a dress.
When she got there,
The cupboard was bare,
And so was her daughter, I guess.

* * *

Little Charles told a sales clerk that he was shopping for a birthday gift for his mother and asked to see some cookie jars.

At the counter with a large selection of jars, he carefully lifted and replaced each lid. At the last one he finally said, "Aren't there any lids that don't make any noise?"

* * *

Did you hear about the little boy who swallowed a quarter, a dime, and a penny?

Asked how he was progressing, the family doctor reported, "There's no change yet."

*   *   *

"Why do you think your Uncle Jack is dumb?"

"You know that sign in the post office that says, 'Man Wanted for Robbery in Oklahoma City'?"

"Yes."

"My uncle went in and applied for the job."

*   *   *

What do you get if you cross a turkey with an ostrich?

A Thanksgiving bird that buries its head in the mashed potatoes.

*   *   *

"Sawyer," scolded the small boy's mother, "your face is clean but how did you manage to get your hands so dirty?"

"Washing my face," replied Sawyer.

*   *   *

Paul Solomon, the Los Angeles science whiz, tells pals this snappy side-splitter:

At the Beverly Hills estate of a motion-picture producer, a small boy's head appeared over the fence and in a meek voice said, "Eh, sir, could I have my arrow back?"

"Certainly, young man," answered the kindly old movie mogul. "Where is it?"

"I think," said the small boy, "that it's stuck in one of your cats."

An Ohio State professor of logic was attempting to teach his young son the principles of clear thinking and the necessity for defining all terms. He pointed to a clock on the wall which had just struck the hour.

"Now if I were to take a hammer and smash the clock," he said, "could I be arrested for killing time?"

"No," said the youngster, "it would be self-defense."

"How do you figure that out?" asked the professor.

"Because," answered the boy, "the clock struck first!"

*   *   *

Dick: What're you doing?

Russ: Writing a letter to my little brother.

Dick: G'wan. You don't know how to write.

Russ: That's O.K. My little brother doesn't know how to read.

*   *   *

"Give me a round trip ticket, please."

"Where to?"

"Back here."

*   *   *

*   *   *

"Did you buy any Christmas Seals?"

"No, I wouldn't know how to feed them."

*   *   *

"Do you like codfish balls?"

"I don't know, I've never been to one."

*   *   *

A five-year-old asked, "Why does it rain, Daddy?"

"To make the flowers grow," said the father, "also the grass, and the trees."

"So why does it rain on the sidewalk?"

*   *   *

Visitor: How old are you, sonny?

Homer: That's hard to say, sir. According to my latest school tests, I have a psychological age of 11 and a moral age of 10. Anatomically, I'm 7; mentally, I'm 9. But I suppose you refer to my chronological age. That's 8—but nobody pays any attention to that these days!

*   *   *

I did my best to show him how,
To hold his lips just so;
I told him to be ready
When I gave the signal *Go!*

He puckered up and closed his eyes
And did what he was told.
It's hard to learn to whistle
When you're only three-years-old!

*　　*　　*

Nobody pays attention to speed limits
these days. The only people you see doing 55
mph on the highway are kids on skateboards.

*　　*　　*

Lawyer Minton was sitting at his desk,
completely absorbed preparing a brief. He
did not hear the door open or see the little
boy come into his office. Attracted by a
sob, Minton looked up and saw a face that
was streaked with tears.

"Well, my little man, did you want to
see me?"

"Are you a lawyer?"

"Yes. What do you want?"

"I want," he stammered, "I want a
divorce from my papa and mama."

*　　*　　*

A mother mosquito and her two daughters were flying over Jones Beach.

"What a wonderful age we live in!" she sighed. "When I was young, the only places you could sting those bathing beauties were the hands and face!"

* * *

"Now, Patrick, aren't you ashamed for having forgotten your pen? What would you call a soldier who went to battle without a gun?"

"A general," piped Patrick.

* * *

Whit: Hey, Todd, where did you get that nice Easter tie?
Todd: What makes you think it's an Easter tie?
Whit: It's got egg on it.

* * *

There once was a young man called Rutter
Who wanted to fly to Calcutta.
 He began with a clang,
 A crash and a bang,
And the farthest he got was the gutter.

* * *

Bobby was the only one in the Staten Island home when the telephone rang.

"Hullo," shouted Bobby.

"Is your father at home?" asked the caller.

"Nobody here 'cept me. I'm Bobby."

"Well, Bobby, will you please tell your daddy that Mr. Quinlin from Seattle called?" Then added, "Perhaps you better write it down."

"OK, wait'll I get a pencil." Bobby had forgotten the man's name so the caller repeated it. "But I can't spell that name," Bobby complained. "It's too hard."

"All right. I'll spell it for you. Q-U-I-N-L-I-N."

There was silence at the other end of the line while Mr. Quinlin fumed. It was certainly taking the boy long enough to write down the seven letters. Finally, Bobby said, "Say, Mister, how do you make a 'Q'?"

184

"Do you understand why Robin Hood robbed only the rich?"

"Sure, because the poor had no money."

*   *   *

One Saturday afternoon Clinton wanted to go to the movies. To find out what picture was playing, he dialed Information, as he had seen his parents do.

"What's the number for the Loew's Theatre?" asked the boy.

The operator gave him the number, and then suggested that perhaps the next time he could find the number in the directory.

"Yes ma'am, I know," explained Clinton, "but I have to stand on the phone book to reach the telephone."

*   *   *

Why did King Kong climb the Empire State Building?

Because he wanted to get his kite.

*   *   *

"What do they call frozen ink?"
"Iced ink."
"You can say that again!"

*   *   *

How can you tell if a vampire has been in your refrigerator?

There'll be two tiny tooth marks in your can of tomato juice.

* * *

Why was Dracula so sleepy?

He kept biting people who had tired blood.

* * *

How do you kill an elephant that's been bitten by a werewolf?

You shoot him through the heart with a silver peanut.

* * *

Trent: That cake you're eating looks good.
Brent: It is good.
Trent: It makes my mouth water.
Brent: To show you what a good guy I am, here's a handkerchief.

* * *

"Do you have any superstitions?"

"No, I don't. I believe it's bad luck to be superstitious."

Eli and Sid were brawling on a Miami street corner when elderly Rabinowitz walked over to them.

"Hey, stop this fighting," said the senior citizen. "Why can't you get along?"

"What do you expect?" replied Eli. "We come from a broken condominium!"

*   *   *

"Did you hear the joke about the rope?"
"No."
"Skip it."

*   *   *

"Tommy, why are you scratching yourself?"

"No one else knows where I itch."

*   *   *

Hugh was playing at Jeffrey's house. When it was time to go home, it started to rain. Jeffrey's mom gave Hugh her son's raincoat and boots.

"You don't have to go to all that trouble," said Hugh politely.

"I'm sure your mother would do as much for Jeffrey," she replied.

"My mom would do more," said Hugh. "She'd ask Jeffrey to stay to supper."

*   *   *

Diana: My mama got a nice present yesterday an' she threw her arms around papa's neck. What does your mama do when she gets a nice present?

Roddy: She tells daddy she'll forgive him, but he mustn't stay out late again.

*   *   *

A newsboy stood on a busy Chicago street corner shouting "Extra! Read all about it! 200 people swindled by offer of pornographic reading material!"

A passerby handed the lad a quarter, grabbed a paper, leafed through it, and growled, "Hey, there's nothing in here about any porno gyp."

The newsboy roared, "Extra! Read all about it! 201 people swindled by offer of pornographic reading material!"

*   *   *

Lucas remarked casually to his wife, "By the way, I hear that our neighbor Mrs. Panelli is pregnant again."

Six-year-old Connie quickly said, "Can't they find out what's causing it?"

*   *   *

San Francisco scholar, Danny Kennedy, is keen on this cooky cackler:

Bouton, the scoutmaster, and some young scouts were sitting around a campfire. He was lecturing the boys on the hazards of camping out. "And, boys," warned Bouton, "you must be careful of snakes. If a snake bites someone on the leg, just take out your knife and crisscross the place where the snake bit him and suck out the poison. Are there any questions?"

"Mr. Bouton," asked young Arnold, "you say if a snake bites someone on the leg you cut it with a knife and suck out the poison? What do you do if a snake bites you on the rear end?"

"Well, Arnold," replied the scoutmaster, "that's when you find out who your friends are."

Jasper, wearing his Boy Scout uniform, was asked by the scoutmaster, "What good deed did you do today?"

"Oh, said Jasper, "Mother had only enough castor oil for one dose, so I let my sister take it!"

*　　*　　*

Corbett, a ten-year-old cub scout, went on a camping trip with his troop. He sent his mother a postcard: *"Yesterday our scoutmaster took us on a mountain-climbing expedition. I wasn't too good so I broke a leg. But don't worry—it wasn't one of mine."*

*　　*　　*

David and Craig, two Boy Scouts whose younger brother had fallen into a pond, rushed home to Mother with tears in their eyes. "We're trying to give him artificial respiration," cried David, "but he keeps getting up and walking away."

*　　*　　*

A pretty girl forgot her fare,
But the bus driver was not rough—
She kissed him sweetly then and there,
And he said, "Fare enough."

*   *   *

Ralph: I went to the zoo yesterday and got in trouble.

Perry: How did you get in trouble?

Ralph: I fed a monkey.

Perry: How did you get in trouble by feeding a monkey?

Ralph: I fed a monkey to a lion.

*   *   *

What do you get when you cross a whale with a penguin?

A submarine in a tuxedo.

*   *   *

What do you get when you cross a praying mantis and a termite?

A bug that says grace before eating your house.

*   *   *

Carol: My brother has a new invention and it's very practical, too.

Barbi: What is it?

Carol: He makes the chickens swim in hot water to lay hard-boiled eggs.

*   *   *

A canny young fisher named Fisher
Once fished from the edge of a fissure.
A fish with a grin
Pulled the fisherman in.
Now they're fishing the fissure for Fisher.

* * *

Did you hear about the near-sighted basketball player who married a giraffe?

* * *

Kelly Bonnett, Rawlins' youngest baseball star, gets giggles from the gang on this goofy gleeful:

Kindall, the father of a Little League baseball player, arrived as the teams were locked in battle. He approached a youngster on the bench and asked, "What's the score?"

"Twenty-eight to nothing."

"Good heavens!" muttered Kendall. "Twenty-eight to zero. Boy, that's real bad!"

"Oh, no, it is not," said the kid. "We haven't been up to bat yet."

* * *

What do you get if you cross a lizard with a baseball player?

An outfielder who catches flies on his tongue and eats them.

What do you get if you cross a tree with a baseball player who hits a lot of home runs?

Babe Root.

*　　*　　*

When Dracula plays baseball, what does he use when it's his turn to hit?

A vampire bat.

*　　*　　*

Murray waited outside Yankee Stadium for his date. She was more than an hour late, and when she finally arrived he was so angry he could hardly speak. Silently, he bought the tickets and they went in. By the time they reached their seats, it was the end of the sixth inning.

"What's the score?" she asked.

"Nothing to nothing," he answered.

"There, you see," she declared. "We haven't missed a thing!"

*　　*　　*

ABOUT THE AUTHOR

LARRY WILDE, the world's bestselling humorist, was born in Jersey City, spent two years in the U.S. Marine Corps and then graduated from the University of Miami (Fla.). He began his career in show business as a standup comedian, playing the nation's nightclubs and theaters and appearing on television commercials and sitcoms.

Mr. Wilde has appeared on the bill with such stars as Ann-Margret, Debbie Reynolds, Pat Boone, and many others. He's done acting roles on *Rhoda, Sanford & Son, Mary Tyler Moore,* and performed on *The Tonight Show, The Merv Griffin Show* and *The Mike Douglas Show.*

He has published two serious works on comedy technique: *THE GREAT COMEDIANS* and *HOW THE GREAT COMEDY WRITERS CREATE LAUGHTER.* Both books are recognized as the definitive works on the subject, and are used as textbooks at various universities.

Mr. Wilde's 28 books are now read in every English-speaking land and have been translated into four other languages. With sales of over 7 million, his "Official" joke books have become the largest-selling humor series in the history of publishing.

Larry Wilde is married to Wyoming writer Maryruth Poulos. Mrs. Wilde is the author of *THE BEST OF ETHNIC HOME COOKING*, as well as the co-author of *HOW TO TELL IF HE'S CHEATING (A Woman's Guide To Men Who Fool Around)*. The Wildes live in Northern California.